P9-DNP-595

ADVANCE PRAISE FOR
SILENT IMPACT

"A wonderful reminder of how our small daily actions can have tremendous effects on the people around us. We cast a shadow each and every day. *Silent Impact* is an inspiration and a fun read."

—JEANNINE M. RIVET, EXECUTIVE VICE PRESIDENT OF UNITEDHEALTH GROUP

"So you think you know Joe Schmit because you share a few minutes with him on KSTP every night? Forget it. What did he learn from the likes of Paul Molitor and Larry Fitzgerald? How about Mike Veeck and his daughter? How did he handle his own fight with cancer? You'll enjoy the stories and the life lessons that go with them."

—DAVE MONA, COHOST WCCO RADIO'S *SPORTS HUDDLE WITH SID AND DAVE*

"Seldom is a 'success' book a page-turner, but this one is. Schmit shares down-to-earth, pragmatic lessons you can immediately begin to implement and benefit from."

—BOB MACDONALD, RETIRED CEO OF ALLIANZ LIFE OF NORTH AMERICA, AUTHOR, AND FOUNDER OF CTW CONSULTING

"I was moved by the powerful examples and their authenticity. *Silent Impact* captures remarkable truths that will benefit and inspire everyone who reads this book."

—DAVID HORSAGER, SPEAKER AND AUTHOR OF
NATIONAL BESTSELLER *THE TRUST EDGE*

"The real-life stories illustrate and confirm how actions, attitudes, behavior, and judgments impact people in ways that can last a lifetime. *Silent Impact* establishes the basis for our most important relationship—the relationship we have with ourselves."

—BILL POPP, POPP COMMUNICATIONS,
LIMITED PARTNER OF THE MINNESOTA TIMBERWOLVES

"Leadership is all about influence; *Silent Impact* is a moving investigation of the many ways leadership reveals itself and how even the smallest of actions can have the greatest influence."

—BILL DUNLAP, RETIRED CHAIRMAN,
CAMPBELL MITHUN; FORMER ASSISTANT
POSTMASTER GENERAL, UNITED STATES OF AMERICA

SILENT IMPACT

STORIES OF **INFLUENCE** THROUGH
PURPOSE, PERSISTENCE, & PASSION

SILENT IMPACT

STORIES OF **INFLUENCE** THROUGH PURPOSE, PERSISTENCE, & PASSION

JOE SCHMIT

SILENT IMPACT © copyright 2014 by Joe Schmit.
All rights reserved. No part of this book may be reproduced in any form
whatsoever, by photography or xerography or by any other means,
by broadcast or transmission, by translation into any kind of language,
nor by recording electronically or otherwise, without permission in
writing from the author, except by a reviewer, who may quote brief
passages in critical articles or reviews.

ISBN 13: 978-1-940014-09-8

Library of Congress Catalog Number: 2013956579

Printed in Canada
Second Printing: 2014
18 17 16 15 14   6 5 4 3 2

Cover and interior design by James Monroe Design, LLC.

Wise Ink, Inc.
53 Oliver Ave S
Minneapolis, MN 55404

www.wiseinkpub.com
To order, visit www.itascabooks.com or call 1-800-901-3480.
Reseller discounts available.

For Laura and our kids,
Natalie, Gaby, and Matthew.

CONTENTS

Introduction | 1

PURPOSE

PERSISTENCE

PASSION

CONTENTS

INTRODUCTION

We make our biggest impressions when we are not trying to be impressive. The words we say or don't say, the things we do or don't do, and the way we react or don't react all work together to make a powerful impact on those around us. It's in our daily interactions that we make either a positive or a negative impact. I call this *Silent Impact*.

The problem is that many of us are sleepwalking through life—not realizing that through both the mundane and monumental moments of life, we are impacting those around us. Sometimes in this busy, crazy, hectic world, we become mesmerized by it all and lose our intentionality. We need to wake up and realize that whether we intend to or not, we are always leaving a mark.

If there were a going-away party tonight, which employee would the most people show up for? We asked that question to small, medium, and even large Fortune 500 companies. The results were remarkable. The people named were often not the ones at the top of the organization. Sometimes the most influential person at work is not the person in the corner office. Sometimes it's the person who *cleans* the corner office.

> *Sometimes the most influential person at work is not the person in the corner office. Sometimes it's the person who cleans the corner office.*

These impact players have more to say about the culture of your company or organization than most leaders suspect. It's not only up to the leaders to find those people, but also to foster their greatness.

The people who were identified in our research as influencers all had certain traits in common. We broke them down into three areas: **Purpose, Persistence, and Passion**.

PURPOSE

Those who had great impact in their workplace aligned their actions with their values. They were genuine. They had integrity and they always put the team in front of themselves.

PERSISTENCE

Those who had great impact in their workplace were persistently positive and also relentless in their preparation. They routinely went above and beyond for everyone on the team—no questions asked.

PASSION

Those who had great impact in their workplace were the heart and soul of the operation. They cared about others as employees, but they also cared about them as people. They knew what was going on in other people's lives, enjoyed their successes, and showed concern over their adversities. They simply always, always cared.

I call these people impact players because of the undeniable influence they have on the world around them. Whether in the home, volunteer organization, church, or workplace, impact players are people who make everyone around them better just by being there. They have great influence in their company's culture and in others' lives. They are gold. That is what we all should strive to be.

Unlike many so-called self-help books, I decided not to use many quotes from people smarter than me. But this quote by the legendary Jackie Robinson is worth our focus. It is the real reason I wrote this book.

"A LIFE ISN'T SIGNIFICANT EXCEPT FOR ITS IMPACT ON OTHER LIVES."
—JACKIE ROBINSON

Read it again and let it soak in. *"A life isn't significant except for its impact on other lives."* How can you be more significant? How can you have a bigger impact on others' lives? Jackie Robinson changed the world when he broke the color barrier in baseball. In the end, it had little to do with baseball and everything to do with helping society change.

INTRODUCTION

One of my favorite Jackie Robinson stories happened when the Brooklyn Dodgers were in Cincinnati, Ohio. Robinson had just committed an error in the field and the racial taunts and mean-spirited slurs had reached a crescendo. Shortstop Pee Wee Reese had heard enough. He went over and stood next to Robinson, put his arm around him, and faced the fans. The fans grew quiet. Later, Robinson said that unselfish act by Reese saved his career. More important than Robinson's career was the strong public message of acceptance of African Americans demonstrated that baseball season. The support and influence of Jackie Robinson's teammates made a powerful impact on baseball fans and on the entire country!

It's a new focus on how you live, work, and play. It's the intersection of two human traits: wanting to be appreciated and wanting to make a difference.

Silent Impact is a new way of thinking about the power of influence and how you can have a positive impact on many. It's a new focus on how you live, work, and play. It's the intersection of two human traits: wanting to be appreciated and wanting to make a difference. With some very simple steps, you can become a person of influence as a parent, as a friend and a colleague, and, more broadly, in your community. Influence is really the ultimate compliment because people will want to be like you and want to follow you.

This book is a collection of stories and vignettes that will help inspire you to have a focused look at influence and how you have an opportunity to make a silent impact on others. Some stories are about people you know and others are about people you don't know. Some stories are personal to me and some are not. Some are long and some are short. The book includes action items that will help you accentuate your influence, be more successful in your job and career, and improve your relationships and overall happiness.

PURPOSE

NO AVERAGE JOE

When Joe Mauer, six-time All-Star for the Minnesota Twins and 2009 American League Most Valuable Player (MVP), was going to Cretin-Derham Hall High School in St. Paul, Minnesota, in the late 1990s, he was the big man on campus. Joe was tall, handsome, and one of the most-talented high school athletes in Minnesota history. He was offered a full-ride scholarship to play quarterback at Florida State, he was an All-State guard in basketball, and he was the best high school baseball player in the country. Drafted by the Minnesota Twins in 2001, Joe Mauer is the only catcher in MLB history to win three batting titles.

In every lunchroom in every high school in the nation, there is a "cool" table where the coolest of the school eat lunch. Whether you sat there or not, you know it's true. Joe Mauer earned a seat at that table, but he didn't choose that table. You see, every day Mauer chose to sit with a classmate who was blind. As a matter of fact, Joe walked Mike Hally from his fourth hour class to the lunchroom, and after lunch, Joe walked him to his next class. Mike was a kid who could have been ignored or shunned because of his disability, but Joe made him one of the cool kids. Imagine the impact it had on Joe's friends and other students at the high school. The ripple effect of Joe's actions in high school is even more impactful now, given his rise to athletic fame. We make our biggest impressions when we are not trying to be impressive.

Reporter's NOTEBOOK*

Over a decade has passed since Joe Mauer invited Mike Hally to sit at a table filled with popular athletes in high school, but the impact is still being felt today. Mike says that no matter how many All-Star games or batting titles Joe wins, he will always think of him as a better person than athlete.

"The act broke down barriers. It gave me confidence to meet other people. Joe taking me to lunch was a sign to all the other athletes that it was okay to be my friend," Mike recalled. Mike also said that his parents feel indebted to Joe for the remarkable way he befriended their son during high school.

One of the best days of the week in the lunchroom was pizza day. Brian Bohlig remembers that after lunch, Joe would make sure that Mike did not have any crumbs on his shirt and would even take a napkin and wipe his face if there was some pizza sauce on it.

> *Joe just cared about other people. It was always about them and not about him.*

"Before we realized it, everyone was doing it. Mike just became one of the guys. I remember that we laughed a lot," Brian recalls. He added, "It was an incredible learning experience. Joe just cared about other people. It was always about them and not about him."

SILENT IMPACT

Tony Leseman is now the Admissions Director of Cretin-Derham Hall High School. He is one of Joe Mauer's best friends and was one of those students who sat at the cool table. Tony said that people should understand that Joe was such a big deal that kids would ask him for his autograph during the school day. "Whatever Joe did spread like wildfire in the school," Tony recalled. "Joe was just Joe, he has no idea the impact he's had." Tony says that Joe wasn't trying to be a hero. Lunch with Mike had to do with Joe's values.

Mike Hally could not see, but you don't need 20/20 vision to see that Joe Mauer is an impact player both on and off the field. I asked Joe why he took Mike to lunch every day. His answer was simple, yet powerful: "Because it was the right thing to do."

*Even in this day and age of technology, journalists still use a reporter's notebook to write down notes when researching a story. Whenever you see a Reporter's Notebook segment in this book, you know that author Joe Schmit used his reporting skills to dig deeper to uncover the lasting impact made in those people's lives.

Reporter's NOTEBOOK PART II

Brother Michael Lee has had hundreds of amazing students over the years at Cretin-Derham Hall High School. When he thinks about the greatest high school athlete he's ever seen, Joe Mauer, he does not think about him for his athletic feats, but rather for his remarkable acts of kindness.

"Joe is the kid who took a blind student to lunch every day and he could do amazing things with any kind of ball, but keep it in that order," stated Brother Michael. He recalls one other poignant moment with Mauer that is consistent with how he treated his blind friend. In one of the classes he was teaching, Brother Michael made each of his students complete the following sentence: "The thing I like about myself the most is . . ." When the unfinished sentence got to Mauer, every person in the classroom, including Brother Michael, expected him to say he liked his athletic skills the most. But here is what Mauer said: "The thing I like about myself the most is that I treat everyone the same. I am nice to everybody."

Brother Michael Lee was so inspired by Mauer's act of maturity and kindness, that he penned a poem called, "Lunch with Mike," which is really a letter from the heart that he wrote late in Joe's senior year. It's personal, poignant, and powerful.

"LUNCH WITH MIKE"

Dear Joe,

We both know that it was infinitely more important than anything you have done or will do with a ball no matter its shape.

For what happened with Mike is who you are and the ball thing is something you do—granted you do it better than 99+ percent of the population.

And many will confuse what you do with who you are and some will insist that you are what you do. That confusion will be theirs, not yours.

And they'll probably pay you to do, but can never buy who you are.

And what you do will probably change now and then in your lifetime, but who you are will not.

And I'm sure there are those who enviously desire to be you, though they really don't know the what or why they seek.

He (Mike) has never seen, will never see what you do and thus, perhaps, see you most clearly.

And there are those who can and do see with eyes only and thus cannot, do not, will not really see you.

And, as for me, I think I'll continue to enjoy seeing what you do; I know I'll always respect, be thankful for, and love who you are.

May you always be and love yourself.

Friend, Brother Michael Lee

KNOW YOUR PURPOSE

I was a freshman in college and had just lived through the typical grueling week of hitting the books. I can actually remember going to the library that week—talk about grueling. About eight of us from my dorm decided we needed to get off campus, so we headed downtown for happy hour. A couple of hours later, we were walking back to our dorm and decided to stop at McDonald's. The eight of us made a mess of our table and left the restaurant.

We made it about a block before we realized that we had lost one of the guys. Where was Gordy? Gordy was one of those guys who joked around with the best of them, but he knew when to reel it in. The truth is that he was probably more mature than any of us. We knew Gordy wasn't just messing around, so we headed back to McDonald's. When we got there, we found Gordy in the restaurant cleaning up our big mess!

"Why are you doing that?" I asked.

He said, "We made the mess. We clean it up. Why am I better than the person who would have to clean this up?"

Reporter's NOTEBOOK

That move by Gordy made a silent impact on me. To this day, when I am in a fast-food restaurant, I clean my table and the one next to me. I do this because of Gordy. My kids do the same thing because of me. You see how this works? Silent impact has a

Align your actions with your values. Isn't that what integrity is all about?

tremendous ripple effect. It's undeniably contagious. Gordy was purposeful. Any other college freshman would have walked out with his friends, leaving the mess for someone else to clean up. Be intentional. Align your actions with your values. Isn't that what integrity is all about?

THE PARENT TRAP

As parents, our integrity gets tested all the time. We make an impact on our children even when we don't think they are watching. Let's say you are with your thirteen-year-old son buying tickets to get into an amusement park. Ages twelve and under costs twenty-five dollars, and thirteen years and above is twice that—a whole fifty bucks! You lean over to your son and say, "You're twelve today." It's a funny and maybe familiar scenario, but for twenty-five dollars, you just sold out on integrity. You just gave your son a gateway to lie whenever he doesn't like the rules, regulations, or even laws.

STATE CHAMP VS. STATE CHUMP

One year, I was covering the Minnesota State Wrestling tournament and there was a very close championship match. The two undefeated wrestlers could not have been more evenly matched. The winner was decided on a last-second controversial call that unbiased fans felt could have gone either way. The kid who lost the match was coming off the mat, looking dejected. I saw his dad walking toward him and thought, *Here comes a Lifesaver commercial moment.* But instead of hugging his son, the father stormed right past him to go give the referee a piece of his mind. He yelled and screamed, making quite a scene. The son wanted to be the state champ; instead the dad became the state chump!

That dad made a silent impact, but it was not positive. Instead of telling his son how proud he was for all his effort and hard work, he sent the message that when things don't go right and life seems unfair, yell, scream, and holler about it. Make no mistake; silent impact can be negative.

IMPACT RESOLUTIONS

I have an easy path for you to become a more influential person. Most people make New Year's resolutions annually and within several weeks they are forgotten. Forget about New Year's resolutions; start doing monthly Impact Resolutions.

Every thirty days, recommit yourself to a resolution that will help make you a person of significant impact. These are not your typical resolutions to lose weight, eat healthier, or quit smoking. This is how I do them: I choose a human trait that I need to work on. It's either a positive trait that I want to be better at or a negative trait that I want to eliminate. I intentionally focus on that trait for the entire month.

For example, my first resolution was to be less petty. Pettiness is something we all feel from time to time. Someone takes credit when you deserve the credit. Someone gets the promotion you should have gotten. Someone else's son is named the captain of the basketball team. If you allow pettiness into your life, you will *be* petty.

So for that month, instead of saying something negative or firing off an e-mail because my emotions were raw, I reminded myself of my resolution. Impact Resolutions really work! Here are some to consider:

Be less judgmental

Give one compliment a day

Be more patient

Smile more

Be more understanding

Listen more than you talk

Be more generous

Be more tolerant

Show more gratitude

I had a friend who picked an accountability partner. She worked in an environment where company gossip was prevalent, so she and her friend decided not to gossip for a month. If one of them gossiped, the other one called them out. When the month ended, boy did they have a lot to talk about!

You could do it as a team at your workplace. Pick twelve traits and map out the year. Get everyone involved and you could impact the culture of your company.

STARR GAZING

Growing up in Wisconsin, you have two choices: become a Packer fan or move. Maybe that's where the famous business book by Spencer Johnson, *Who Moved My Cheese*, came from. Like many kids who grew up in Dairyland, I loved Jesus, cheese, and the Green Bay Packers. My favorite Packer was always Bart Starr, the Hall of Fame quarterback who was the MVP of the first two Super Bowls. Little did I know that Bart Starr would have a silent impact on this sports-crazy kid from Seymour, Wisconsin.

By the time I went to college, Starr had retired from being a player and was the head coach of the Packers. I was majoring in broadcasting, and I was sure I would get an easy A on a class project if I could somehow finagle an interview with Coach Starr. What luck! I was able to set up a fifteen-minute interview with the Packers coach while I was on Christmas break. One of my best friends at college, John "Mac" MacGregor, was a broadcasting major specializing in photojournalism. He lived in Appleton, Wisconsin, which was just thirty miles from Green Bay, so he would be able to shoot the interview.

Lee Remmel, the longtime public relations director and sports writer of the Green Bay Packers, made it clear that the coach was busy and we would only have fifteen minutes with him. I am not sure who was more nervous, Mac or me. Coach Starr was gracious and patient, and I made sure we were done within our allotted time limit.

When we were done, I thanked Coach Starr and he said, "Gentlemen, are you in a hurry?" I quickly replied that we were not in a hurry. "Then why don't I give you a tour of the Packers facility?" he said. Before we knew it, we were in the green and gold Packers locker room. We went into the weight room, meeting rooms, and even got to see the two Vince Lombardi Trophies Starr helped the team win.

Mac and I were both amazed that Coach Starr would take the time for two college kids who were more than elated just to land a fifteen-minute interview. I would later find out that this was not a rare occurrence for Bart Starr. He was a man who understood the power of purpose. He took the extra time to give two college kids an experience they would never forget.

Reporter's NOTEBOOK

Fast-forward four years and I was covering the Green Bay Packers for WBAY-TV in Green Bay. That meant that I was covering Coach Bart Starr on a daily basis. Although Starr was never able to match the success as a coach that he had as a player, he was still very much an impact player.

When my dad died in 1983, Starr and the Packers sent flowers to the funeral home. *First class* and *Bart Starr* were once again synonymous. I went back to work about a week after the funeral and attended a Bart Starr news conference. When the session wrapped up, Starr said, "Joe, can I see you for a moment?"

We went back to an empty office where he gave me his deepest sympathies. But then, the coach took the next step. He said, "Joe, tell me about your dad." I told him a few things and then he told me about his dad. We talked for the next ten or fifteen minutes about how much our dads meant to us. Bart Starr simply cared and by taking time out of an extremely busy schedule to show it, he made an impact on me.

STARRY, STARRY NIGHT

The 1983 season did not go very well for the Green Bay Packers and their beleaguered head coach, Bart Starr. The Packers were playing a game on Monday Night Football in the Meadowlands against the New York Giants. This was pretty much a do-or-die game for the Packers. They needed to win the game to remain in the play-off hunt. A loss meant no play-offs and most likely an end to Bart Starr's coaching job.

I was the sports director for WBAY-TV in Green Bay. Back in those days, the media flew on the team's charter plane. After a difficult loss, we landed in Green Bay at about two thirty in the morning right in the middle of a snowstorm. It was cold, windy, and snowing—weather that was extreme even by Green Bay standards.

There is one road from Austin Straubel International Airport back to the city of Green Bay. All forty players along with the coaches, trainers, front office personnel, and media would take on this "frozen tundra" kind of night. As everyone on the flight left the airport, there was a stalled car with a guy trying to change his tire in the ugly conditions. Not one person stopped to help the poor guy. The man did notice a white station wagon slow down to take a peek, but then took off toward Green Bay like all the other vehicles.

This story might have never been told, but I later found out that the guy with the stalled vehicle was one of my high school classmates. In fact, his sister was my high school girlfriend. When the white station wagon returned a short time later to help out, it was Bart Starr. He had gone home to drop off his wife and pick up some warm clothes. Then, he went back to help change the tire.

Reporter's NOTEBOOK

Of all the people on that airplane who could have or should have stopped to help, Bart Starr was the least likely candidate. But when you are an impact player in life, you go above the call of duty even when no one is looking. That's what character is all about and that is what making an impact is all about. You simply care for people.

Bart Starr was fired after that season. I hosted a half-hour show called "Bart Starr: The Player, The Coach, The Man." I could have talked about Starr's charity work or his dedication to his wife Cherry, but I told the snowstorm story. I am sure there are hundreds if not thousands more stories just like it because Bart Starr cared. I have made my fair share of mistakes in my life, but picking Bart Starr as my idol as a kid was a rock-solid choice.

> "Use what you got
> to get what you want."
> —Mike McKinley

Hall of Fame speaker Mike McKinley said this to me as I was ramping up my speaking and seminar business. It makes so much sense, but sometimes people step out of their comfort zone and get away from what made them successful in the first place. If you are a serious-minded person, you probably don't want to be a stand-up comic. Know your strengths and your weaknesses and use what you got to get what you want. By doing so, you will be a positive influence on others!

YOU'VE GOTTA HAVE FRIENDS

One of the best lines that I've heard about friendship goes like this: A good friend will bail you out of jail, but your best friend will sit next to you and say, "Damn that was fun." That might be a little extreme, but I think you get the idea.

You can tell how good of a friend you have by how much influence they have over you. If your friend tells you about a fantastic restaurant or a great movie, do you go without question? Do you go to your friend with good news only, or do you also call him or her when things go badly?

The older I get, the more I realize that maintaining meaningful relationships takes work. We are all busy and we have many options, but having close friends who will level with you is very healthy. Some people develop their personal board of directors to help guide them through the hardest challenges of life. I have quite a few circles of friends and that works well for me. I have my closest buddies with whom I golf and fish. Our extended families are close. I have my professional friends, both in TV and in the speaking business. I have my lifelong friends who I don't get to see very often, but when we are together, it's comfortable right away. We have history together. It's friendship equity and it's priceless. Friends can be a major influence on your life and career. Pick them wisely, continue to invest in the relationships, and maybe you will have a bunch of best friends sitting in that jail cell with you.

A FATHER'S GIFT

During the formative years of my life, I grew up in a bar. "That might explain a few things," my friend teases. This bar was in Seymour, Wisconsin. Seymour's claim to fame is being the "Home of the Hamburger." In 1885, Charles Nagreen began calling ground-beef patties in a bun "hamburgers." That same year, Hamburger Charlie sold his soon-to-be famous burgers at the Seymour Fair. To this day, Seymour, Wisconsin, enjoys an annual celebration called Hamburger Days. You haven't truly lived until you experience the ketchup slide competition!

Some small towns have a café where everybody goes to find out what's happening. In Seymour, the American Legion Club was that place and my dad ran it. The social hub of Seymour, it's where the "Who's Who" of Seymour wanted to be seen. It was like the old TV show, *Cheers*—"Sometimes you want to go where everybody knows your name."

We lived in the house connected to the Legion, making it convenient to do chores for my dad. Before we went to school every morning, my brothers and I would clean the bar, wash the ashtrays, empty the bottle chute of all the beer bottles from the night before, and separate the bottles for reuse. We were recycling before we knew what recycling was! Because of my daily chores, I went to school every day smelling like stale beer and cigarette butts.

It was a family business. It wasn't 24/7/365, but it was open most of the time. It opened at eight o'clock in the morning because when the farmers finished milking their cows, it was their happy hour. They'd come in for a shot of whiskey or a beer and good conversation with Smitty, the guy behind the bar.

The American Legion Club revolved around my dad. He knew everybody in town and everybody in town knew him. More than that, my dad knew how to make lasting connections with people. There is no doubt that when he was bartending, people stayed longer. My dad could have written the book on customer service. In other words, he was a man of influence. He was short in stature but long in personality. His gift was making people feel better about themselves through his energy and humor.

His gift was making people feel better about themselves through his energy and humor.

There was one guy who became my dad's best friend. His name was Mr. Liesch. They were like brothers. Mr. Liesch was the local soda distributor, so he was at the bar often. When he would visit, my dad often gave me quarters to play the jukebox or pinball machine. After this happened several times, I realized that my dad was just trying to get me away from the bar so he could tell Mr. Liesch a dirty joke. I did get in trouble once for repeating one of those jokes that I overheard. I had no idea what it meant, but I wanted to make people laugh, just like my dad. My classmates didn't get the joke either, but when one of my friends went home and repeated the joke to his parents, I was in *trouble*.

Since Seymour was a town of around 2,500 people, it had a volunteer fire department and my dad was a volunteer firefighter. The Legion was one of three places that could sound the fire siren for our town, so we got a lot of phone calls. One day we got a call that I knew was different. I'll never forget the look on my dad's face. I could see the fear in his eyes, and it scared me. When he hung up the phone, he immediately called out for my mom and then he left. I had never seen my dad react like that and I knew right away it was not good news.

My dad's closest friend, Mr. Liesch, had been killed in a car accident. I don't remember a lot about the next few days, but I do remember that I never saw my dad cry. He was "old school"; men didn't show their emotions. I knew the grief was overwhelming, and I do recall my mom telling me that my dad cried it out behind closed doors.

After the initial shock and grief settled, my dad had a clear vision of his new purpose. His job as a best friend did not end when Mr. Liesch died. You see, Mr. Liesch needed my dad more than ever. Mr. Liesch had a son named Donnie who was only one year younger than me. From that point forward, Donnie was one of four boys jammed in the back seat of our Ford Galaxy, joining us for family trips and events.

There were already six kids in our family, Donnie made seven. Yes, we were good Catholics. Back in those days, the Catholics had rhythm and they had bingo. If you didn't have rhythm . . . BINGO! Dad made sure that Donnie would come with us to picnics, hockey games, and baseball games. I remember complaining to my big brothers about Donnie always tagging along. I wasn't old enough to understand what my dad was doing for Donnie.

During my college and early broadcasting years, I lost track of Donnie. To be completely honest, I didn't think about him much for many years. The next time I saw Donnie, he was crying. The occasion was extremely sad for me also. It was my dad's funeral. I was overwhelmed with grief and don't remember much from that day. I didn't fully process what I observed until about a decade later when I became heavily involved in the Big Brothers Big Sisters organization. I had been a Big Brother through their mentorship program since before my dad died, and I was now serving on the board of directors and helping raise awareness and funds for this phenomenal organization.

Each summer for sixteen years, I organized a charity golf tournament to support Big Brothers Big Sisters. My entire family supported this over the years by attending the event. After the tournament one year, Bob Mitchell, the executive director of Big Brothers said, "Joe, I've met your mom and your brothers and sisters. Tell me about your dad."

I said, "Oh, Bob, you would have loved my dad." And as I started telling Bob about my dad, I drew a connection that I had not drawn before. For the first time, I got it. My dad was a big brother to Donnie! He did not have an organization behind him. He was doing it with his heart. He had a new purpose when his best friend, Mr. Liesch, died. When Donnie lost my dad, he lost the second most influential man in his life.

It occurred to me that my dad's relationship with Donnie was the reason I felt drawn to get involved with Big Brothers Big Sisters. In other words, my dad's actions made a silent impact on me. His influence had a ripple effect. In turn, I was able to become a Big Brother to someone else. Plus, the funds raised in the golf event were used to match more caring, responsible adults to children and teens at risk. One will never know how many people were impacted by my dad's powerful example.

Reporter's NOTEBOOK

My Little Brother from the Big Brothers Big Sisters mentoring program is now in prison in Iowa. Before you judge my mentoring skills, Jim is a prison guard at a prison in Iowa! I mentored Jim in the 1980s and it is my joy to stay in contact with Jim and his family. In the late 1980s, I was invited to a family baptism where I met Jim's second cousin. She is now the mother of my three children. Laura and I have been married since 1989. I am not

When you amplify your purpose, you are aligning your actions with your values.

sure fate would have put us together without my dad's inspiration to step up and make a difference in the life of a child.

When you amplify your purpose, you are aligning your actions with your values. Without realizing it, my dad taught me an amazing lesson. When you give of yourself and expect nothing in return, amazing things can happen. What a remarkable gift and legacy you can leave by making a silent impact in someone's life.

Maya Angelou, poet laureate, says, "People won't remember what you said. People won't remember what you did. But they will remember how you made them feel."

Donnie and I recently reconnected, and we talked about our dads. Donnie admitted he still misses his dad to this day, more than forty-five years since the tragic accident. And guess what, he still misses my dad, too. Donnie said that my dad used to tell him stories about his dad. Donnie relayed such tidbits as, "My dad was always the life of the party. He was the guy who would literally wear the lampshade on his head. No wonder our dads got along so well!" He went on to say, "Those stories really carried me through those years because the pain of Dad's loss didn't go away."

Donnie remembers my dad cheering for him at Little League and Babe Ruth baseball games. I had to admit that I remembered that too and that I was jealous because it seemed my dad would cheer more loudly for Donnie than for me. Donnie says that my dad helped him get a job at the Seymour Canning Company. He said my dad would swing by to check on him and tell him a joke now and then to get him to laugh.

"Your dad filled a spot in a time that I really needed someone. I had uncles I would see, but your dad was different. He had a special role in my life, like the times he visited me because my mom told him I was acting out. Your dad would come and visit me, we'd sit down and talk about it, and everything would be okay again for a while."

I am so thankful for my father's gift to Donnie. He left a legacy of silent impact that took me years to fully recognize. What my dad did for two boys from Seymour, Wisconsin, lives in both of us today.

DON'T BURY THE LEAD

In the news business, there is a saying that is used often: "Don't bury the lead." For example, you would not start a story on the Super Bowl by writing: "The Super Bowl was played this year in the Superdome in New Orleans. Over 90,000 fans were in attendance to see the Baltimore Ravens play the San Francisco 49ers." Your lead is: "The Baltimore Ravens defense gave up 31 points, but a dominating late goal line stand led the Ravens over the San Francisco 49ers, 34-31 in Super Bowl XLVII."

What is *your* lead story? Do you bury the lead? Are you not as influential as you could be because you get caught up in minutia? Mark LeBlanc, former president of the National Speakers Association, believes that too many people spend too much time "getting ready to get ready." It's worth thinking about.

Do you spend time doing what is most important? Do you take care to communicate efficiently and effectively? Are you committed to focusing on what is important to your legacy?

INTENTIONAL IMPACT

There is a TV station in Denver, Colorado, that uses a unique strategy for hiring new photographers. This station is known for its award-winning photo-journalism. Think of them as the New York Yankees of television photography. They gather the best talent money can buy because they know that powerful video will help their reporters tell more compelling stories for their viewers.

In the television business, you are hired off of your résumé tape. For example, a photojournalist would put their greatest hits on a DVD and send them to the station's chief photographer. If the chief photographer is impressed and the candidate's references check out, the candidate will be invited to come in for an interview.

At this station in Denver, they have the candidate do a traditional interview with the chief photographer and the news director. Then they send the candidate out in the field for a day with one of the photographers currently on staff. They spend all day on a story so the candidate and the current employee can get to know each other.

The next day, the second interview takes place. The interview is not with the candidate, but rather with the station's photographer. The photojournalist who spent the day with the candidate is the person answering the questions. The chief photographer and the news director want to know what the candidate said about the TV station he or she is working at now. What did he say about the reporters he currently works with? What questions did he or she ask about the Denver TV station? The candidate's competence is a topic, but not the focus.

The answers to these questions are far more valuable than the candidate's formal interview the day before. If the candidate complained about his or her current station, the news management, or the hours he or she works, the candidate does not get the job. It's as simple as that. The brass at this Denver TV station is smart enough to realize that if the candidate complains about his or her experience at the current station, history will repeat itself in Denver.

These days, when NFL scouts are doing due diligence on college players who they may potentially draft; they look at much more than just players' statistics and athletic abilities. The best scouts will talk to the equipment managers and the student trainers for insight on the player. If the player treats people at all levels of the organization with respect, those behaviors will continue. The prospective employee, without realizing it, will either have a positive or a negative influence on his or her future.

MAMMA'S BOY

My mother became a widow at the age of fifty-two. When my dad died, he had a $10,000 life-insurance policy. I remember my mom worrying about not having anything left to pass on to her six kids when she died.

My mother had an eighth-grade education. She was forced to quit school in order to work to help support her family in the post-Depression years. She did not want to quit school, but back then, that's what Grandpa and Grandma had to do to survive. The family survived the Depression and a polio outbreak that hit three of her twelve siblings, killing one of her brothers. She can remember kids walking past her house putting their hands over their nose and mouth because they were afraid of contracting polio.

My mom married my dad when she was eighteen years old. They had seven children, one of whom died in a late-term miscarriage. She worked various jobs the entire time she raised six kids. She sewed, cooked, cleaned, and ran the family while my dad worked long hours. She made every birthday and holiday special, even if she was pinching pennies to make it happen. We did not have a lot when we grew up, but my mom made sure we never felt like we were without.

When my mom passes, she will not have any money to leave the kids and grandkids, but she will leave us with something worth much more . . . her values. I am thankful for my mom's sense of purpose in life. She never lost sight of her commitment to provide for her children's physical and emotional well-being. My mom has made a positive impact in the lives of her kids and grandkids!

PERSISTENCE

GIVE ME THE GOOD STUFF

I don't know about you, but I like to take nice, long showers. Sometimes I am in there so long I can't remember if I shampooed my hair, so I do it again just in case. As I have gotten older, I have the same issue as a lot of men . . . I don't need as much shampoo anymore!

In the spring of 2008, while in the shower, I noticed that I had a lump on my chest. I thought it was strange—strange enough that I went to see my doctor about it. He said, "Joe, don't worry. It's probably just a fatty deposit, but just to be safe, why don't you go see a specialist." So I went to another doctor who told me the same exact thing. It was a fatty deposit. He said he could remove it, but I might want to check with my insurance company first because it could be considered cosmetic surgery and therefore not covered by insurance. I told him if he was going to remove fat from my body, we would start in a couple of other places first!

I truly did not think much about it for another month. I just thought I was growing a third boob. About three months later, I celebrated my big five-zero with one of those two-day, in-depth, full-body physicals at Mayo Clinic in Rochester, Minnesota. The world-famous doctors at Mayo are so thorough that they found parts of my body that I did not know I had!

Mayo assigned me to a primary doctor who took a look at my man-boobs, of which I now had three. He agreed with the previous doctors that it was just a fatty deposit. So now I had three guys with decades of combined medical training and experience singing the Bobby McFerrin classic, "Don't Worry, Be Happy."

On the second day of my physical, the doctor spoke to me before my release and said, "Let's be safe, Joe. Let me take a biopsy on that bump before you go." I had the biopsy and did not worry about it. As a matter of fact, it was the opening weekend for fishing in Minnesota. I had plans to fish on one of Minnesota's ten thousand lakes and drink beer with some buddies . . . not necessarily in that order.

A few days after my fishing adventure, I was sitting in my office when I got a call from the doctor at Mayo Clinic. I knew right away the doctor wasn't calling me to find out how many fish I caught. It was the call nobody ever wants to receive. The doctor said that I had non-Hodgkin's lymphoma. He explained that it's a blood cancer that I would have the rest of my life. He said, "Joe, you can beat this thing, but it's not going to be easy." He explained that I was looking

I now had a new mission. Remission was my mission.

at two and a half years of chemotherapy. At that moment, my life changed forever. I now had a new mission. Remission was my mission.

I hung up the phone, closed the door to my office, and took a deep breath. At one time or another, I guess we all wonder how we would react to news of this magnitude. I was surprised that I was neither scared nor mad. But then the nerves set in. I realized that I needed to start telling people and that made me feel very nervous. I called my wife and told her I'd be home for lunch because I wanted to tell her in person. I knew she would need a hug, and I certainly knew that I needed one.

When I got home, I was short and to the point. "Laura, Mayo called and I have lymphoma. We will beat this thing." We hugged, and we quickly did what most people do when they find out devastating medical news. We hopped on the computer and Googled non-Hodgkin's lymphoma. The Internet certainly had to know more about this disease than some experienced doctor at one of the greatest medical institutions in the world. We soon came to our senses and trusted what the Mayo doctor told us.

When you get cancer, the one thing they don't tell you is how to tell your kids. At that time, my kids were fifteen, thirteen, and ten. As parents, from the time they are born, we are there to protect our children. We tell them, "Don't be afraid. There is no such thing as the boogieman." Let me tell you something: cancer *is* the boogieman.

At first we were going to call a family meeting, but we later decided that didn't feel right. We would tell our kids one at a time. Our oldest, Natalie, the emotional type, wanted to hug it out and cry it out. Our middle daughter, Gaby, the new teenager said, "How's this, like, cancer stuff going to, like, affect me?"

Our youngest and only son put his hand up the minute we said the word *cancer*. He did not want to hear any more. A week later, we knew he was processing the news because he asked his mom, "When Dad loses all his hair, will it grow back?" We knew we had to watch all three kids closely, as this would be a tough season for all of us.

The next week, Laura and I headed back down to Mayo Clinic for a series of tests. The music in the waiting room was the theme from *Love Story*. Remembering the tragic storyline of that classic movie, I turned to Laura and said, "This is not a good sign." That is an old movie, but I remember that it was one of the saddest movies ever made. The second waiting room we were in that day, Barbara Streisand was singing "Memories." For my third test of the day, and strike me down if I am lying, the song in the waiting room was Louis Armstrong singing "What a Wonderful World," *another funeral song.* Later, as Laura and I were waiting for the elevator, I said, "If Josh Groban is on this elevator singing 'You Raise Me Up,' we are getting the heck out of here!"

So after all the tests were completed, we met with my oncologist, Dr. Letendre. He's a short French Canadian with a dry sense of humor. The walls in his office were filled with various medical degrees and awards, giving me confidence in his background and ability. He said, "Joe, your cancer is slow moving. If you can live with the idea of cancer in your body, why don't you wait until the fall to start treatment? Your kids will be busy in school and when you get knocked down, it won't be as noticeable to them." I agreed to this plan and Dr. Letendre sent us on our way to enjoy our summer.

As we drove home from Mayo that day, I felt a strong resolve to do everything I could to get ready for chemo. I had about one hundred days to prepare my body for the devastating effects of treatment. I decided I would pretend I was trying out for the high-school football team. That meant I had to get my fifty-year-old self into some serious shape. I hired a personal trainer and got after it. I went from being able to do seventeen push-ups to doing sixty-one push-ups. I was doing seventy-five minutes on the elliptical three or four times a week. I often gave myself personal pep talks to keep the momentum going. When lifting weights, I would push myself on the last few repetitions by saying, "Can cer . . . can . . . not . . . live . . . here." By September, I could have made the high school football team!

I returned to Mayo Clinic for some re-testing before meeting with Dr. Letendre. As I nervously waited, more funeral music was playing over the speakers. *Why do they play this stuff?* I wondered. Expecting a plan of action, complete with the chemo schedule, I was surprised to hear my doctor tell me that the cancer was not moving or growing! He said, "Joe, it has subsided. I'm not going to treat you right now."

I sat there in total silence, thinking, *What the heck?* I had just spent the last one hundred days of my life preparing for this and now I am not going to receive treatment? Call me crazy, but I was ticked off. I was really upset. I was so prepared to fight this cancer that I did not know how to handle such great and unexpected news. You'll be happy to know that after the news sunk in, I was doing cartwheels down the hallways of Mayo Clinic.

I continued to live a full life between my regularly scheduled scans. Two years later, I could tell that things had changed. I wasn't quite feeling like myself. The cancer had started to move. Instead of getting the planned combination of five drugs for my chemotherapy, I was now going to get two. Instead of getting the expected two and a half years of treatment, I was going to have six months. It was another revelation; the millions of dollars spent on research made this new, minimal treatment possible.

A chemo ward could never be confused for Disney World. It is not the happiest place on earth after all. To Mayo's credit, they do everything they can to make it bright and cheery. Even so, there is a reality you face when you are in that room. Everyone there is a member of a club they did not sign up for.

One day while waiting for my chemo treatment, there was a woman sitting next to me waiting for her treatment as well. When the nurse came with her bags of chemo, the woman announced for all to hear, "Here comes my poison." I thought to myself, *Wow, she has it all wrong.*

So when the nurse came with my bag of chemo, I declared, "Here comes the good stuff. Give me the good stuff; the good stuff gets rid of the bad stuff." I was very aware of the power of preparing my mind as well as my body for this intense treatment. Four months after I started chemo, my cancer was in remission. Remission was my mission and my mission was accomplished!

> *Here comes the good stuff. Give me the good stuff; the good stuff gets rid of the bad stuff.*

Reporter's NOTEBOOK

What I did on my cancer journey was amplify my persistence. I made the decision to go "all in." I knew it was a marathon, not a sprint. It takes mental toughness to be persistent. It takes even more mental toughness to remain persistently positive when faced with tough circumstances.

I really found out about the power of the mind when I was sitting in my doctor's office that day when he told me I didn't need chemo. I was blindsided by my feelings. It surprised me that good news could feel like bad news. How could I be so mad at the news that I would not need chemotherapy? My mind was equipped and ready because I was all in. I've read about soldiers who go through months of training to go to war, and then when they don't get to see battle, they are actually disappointed. Nobody was going to be shooting at me, but I understood the feelings of those soldiers.

SILENT IMPACT

Through this process, I learned to be
continually aware of the people and the
opportunities around me. Our decision to tell
the kids about my cancer individually rather
than in a family meeting was a good example
of this. Everyone handles adversity and tough
times differently. Laura and I were able to help
our kids process this unwanted news in their
own way and in their own time. It was one of
the many lessons learned while on my cancer
journey. We all have those aha-moments. These
moments change who we are and they ultimately
change the impact we have on others around us.

Sometimes the impact you can have on others
is not so silent. "Bring me the good stuff," was
an out-loud statement meant to overcome the
woman's words, "Here comes my poison," that were
still lingering in the air of that waiting room.
It was my way of staying persistently positive.
I hope it also had an impact on the others there
that day. How we choose to approach both the
monumental and mundane moments of life has
impact. I am not brazen enough to say that my
attitude and my approach cured my cancer. I still
have non-curable cancer. What I know for certain

is that my willingness to turn up the dial on persistence made both a physical and mental difference in my battle against cancer.

PICTURE PERFECT

My wife and I have a friend who has a photogenic quality that makes us envious. Teri always looks wonderful in pictures. Her smile is consistent, genuine, and radiant. So one time, I admitted to Teri that my wife and I have marveled at this quality. To my surprise, Teri told me that she used to take terrible pictures. One day, she decided to improve this by changing her mindset. Teri tells herself before every picture, "I am beautiful." It calms her down, perks up her confidence, and she ends up looking marvelous in pictures. So I tried this theory out, except I thought to myself, *I am Brad Pitt.* Now it hasn't worked out yet, but there was one picture out on Facebook where I swear I looked like a chubby Johnny Depp. It doesn't have to be something as big as cancer to exercise the power of your mind. It can be as simple as a Kodak moment.

> "LUCK FAVORS THE PREPARED."
>
> —USHER

Stemming from a Louis Pasteur quote and other ancient and wise proverbs, Usher spoke these words as a way of telling young people that there are no short-cuts. Hard work and persistent preparation are needed to get to the top, no matter what industry. Because of Usher's profile and success, those words and his actions have impact. A few years back, Usher took an unknown singer with a lot of talent and ambition under his wing. Justin Bieber was both prepared and lucky!

THE BALL BOY

Several years ago, I was doing a TV show live from Minnesota State University–Mankato, where the Minnesota Vikings hold training camp each summer. I had a live half-hour TV show at ten thirty that night with my guest for the show, head coach at the time, Denny Green. We were doing the show from the stadium at ten thirty at night and had all of the lights on. Just before we went on the air, one of the Vikings' ball boys, a high-school kid, began running the stairs.

I thought, *This kid just wants some airtime. He probably called some of his buddies and said, "Hey watch channel five tonight, and you will see me in the background running the stadium steps."* Not only did he run the steps, he did so for the entire show!

The next night, I was doing my show from in front of the Vikings' dormitory. The dorm was about a block away from the football field and two blocks away from the hotel where I was staying that night. After my show, I was walking back to the hotel. As I passed the football stadium, I noticed a sound coming from the dark stadium. It sounded something like *ch . . . ch . . . ch* and then at a faster rate, *ch-ch-ch-ch-ch*. I thought, *No way.* I went back and peered through the darkness to see the ball boy running the stairs just as fast as he had the night before during my broadcast. There were no TV cameras or NFL head coaches watching. Nobody was watching.

The ball boy who was running those stairs signed a $120-million contract with the Arizona Cardinals! His name is Larry Fitzgerald Jr. He is one of the best receivers in the entire NFL. After more than ten years in the pros, he is still one of the hardest working players in football. When your best player is a persistent hard worker, you have yourself an impact player.

One hundred twenty million dollars . . . that's a lot of *ch-ch*-ching!

THE HIT PARADE

Another impact player is baseball Hall of Famer Paul Molitor. I was lucky enough to be in Kansas City, Missouri, the night that he became the twenty-first player in Major League history to get his three thousandth hit. It was a monumental accomplishment and a privilege to witness history in the making. The next day, I was at the ballpark early working on logistics with the satellite truck engineer and my cameraman. To our surprise, Paul Molitor walked by us. I said, "Molly, what are you doing here so early?"

He replied, "I came for some early batting practice. I don't like the way I am swinging the bat." Is there any doubt in your mind how he got those first three thousand hits? "Good enough" wasn't good enough because he wanted to be the best. Talk about making a silent impact! The people who normally come in for early batting practice are the

"Good enough" wasn't good enough because he wanted to be the best.

rookies and reserves trying to earn more playing time. Imagine the silent impact it had on those players when history-making Paul Molitor stepped into the batting cage early the next day. Like Larry Fitzgerald Jr., Paul Molitor was being persistent with his preparation.

Reporter's NOTEBOOK

There is a lesson in this for all of us. Do you settle for good enough when you know you could perform better? What silent impact does that make on those around you? On the other hand, what if we were persistently seeking to be on top of our game even when we *are* on top of our game? What silent impact would *that* make?

> *Do you settle for good enough when you know you could perform better?*

THE WISDOM OF WOODEN

I promised you that this book would not be filled with quotes, so when I do use a quote, it has to be profound. John Wooden impacted many through the years. He was a three-time All-American basketball player and was UCLA's head coach, leading them to ten NCAA championships in a twelve-year period! The best way to measure a person's impact is not only what they did when they were alive but what lessons they left after they are gone. John Wooden was one of those guys. He passed away in 2010, leaving behind words of wisdom such as this:

"IT'S WHAT YOU LEARN
AFTER YOU KNOW IT ALL THAT COUNTS."
—JOHN WOODEN

There is a lot to chew on in those eleven words. We live in an ever-changing world with technology, politics, business, values, and so much more. If you are not a lifelong learner or lifelong improver, you are going to get passed by, run over, and left behind.

Look at 3M, the Minnesota-based company that is famous for inventing the Post-it Note. 3M has invented and improved literally millions of products that have improved our lives for years. Their secret is pretty simple. They get most of their ideas from customer complaints. In other words, they are listening, learning, and improving—all the time.

FUN IS GOOD

Mike Veeck is one of the most creative and unique marketing wizards in baseball. He is part-owner and operator of several minor league baseball teams, including the St. Paul Saints. The Saints have been featured in *Sports Illustrated* and *60 Minutes* for their over-the-top promotions. At every Saints game, you can get a haircut or a massage from a nun! They have a pig that brings baseballs out to the umpire during each game too! Mike even had a mime night where mimes would stand on top of the dugout and perform instant replays for the fans. By the way, Mike has written a book called, *Fun is Good: How to Create Joy and Passion in Your Workplace and Career*. It's the motto for everyone who works for the Saints.

One night, I was emceeing a charity event that Mike was attending. I have known Mike for years and I could tell something was wrong. He was just off. I asked him if everything was okay. He replied, "No, it's not. I just found out that my eleven-year-old daughter is going blind." The news was devastating, and I had nothing to say to comfort him. Nothing at all.

Mike and Libby Veeck's daughter Rebecca had been diagnosed with Retinitis Pigmentosa, a degenerative eye disease that has no cure. Rebecca was going to lose her sight.

As tragic as the situation was for the Veecks, the way they handled it was creative, unique, and inspirational. Mike figured out that fun is good even when life circumstances are not. Sometimes you have to laugh to overcome fear. The Veecks allowed me to document Rebecca's story on television and show how the family was dealing with the stark reality that their precious girl was going blind.

As the Veecks did research on blindness, they discovered that people who have sight but lose it remember everything they have seen in vivid detail after they lose their vision. So the Veecks decided they had to let Rebecca see things they deemed important. They traveled to Washington, DC, to see the monuments. They went to the Grand Canyon. They went to the Baseball Hall of Fame in Cooperstown, New York, so she could see her grandfather's plaque. Mike's father was the legendary Bill Veeck who owned several baseball teams. He once sent three-foot-seven-inch Eddie

Gaedel to the plate in a real game in 1951. Rebecca also saw Gaedel's jersey in the hall of fame. He wore the number 1/8. The apple did not fall far from the tree. Classic Veeck!

Mike Veeck was working for the Tampa Bay Devil Rays at the time we took footage for this story. We were with him when he put Rebecca on his lap and let her drive around the vacant parking lot in his convertible. I'll never forget the smile on Rebecca's face as she turned the steering wheel with the wind in her hair. It was a father–daughter moment that came prematurely. Mike said, "This is probably not the best parenting, but I want her to know what it is like to drive a car." Mike and Rebecca also came up with a song about Retinitis Pigmintosa. The Veecks could not change the prognosis for their daughter, but they could alter the way she would see the world, even in darkness.

> *This is probably not the best parenting, but I want her to know what it is like to drive a car.*

Sometimes you have to be intentional with your influence. Little did I know that the way this family handled their crisis would have an impact on me when I was diagnosed with cancer.

Reporter's NOTEBOOK

Rebecca is now in her twenties and plans to move into her own apartment after going to the Conklin Center for the blind in Florida, a place designed to teach visually impaired people how to live independently. Her goal is to get a job and live on her own. Rebecca's journey has not been easy. Her mother says that Rebecca has a hard time accepting that she has limitations, but she has embraced the technology needed to adapt to living without sight. For example, Rebecca has a device that can read the bar code on food labels so she knows that she is opening a can of soup, not a can of dog food!

Mike, Libby, and Rebecca seek to make an influence. They have given much time and energy to annual fundraisers in partnership with the minor league baseball team in Charleston, South Carolina, the RiverDogs. Their fundraisers benefit Storm Eye Institute, a part of the Medical University of South Carolina.

When we told Rebecca's story on KSTP-TV in 2000, my photographer, Joe Caffrey, and I both had daughters her age. This was a hard story to tell because it hit close to home. We felt compelled to show the magnitude of courage coming from the Veeck family. Joe and I won an Emmy for the story. After an extremely short discussion, we sent the Emmy statuette to Rebecca. After all, she deserved it more than we did.

NEGATING NEGATIVITY

Persistence requires keeping a positive perspective, especially when times are tough. One of the best ways to stay positive is to limit your exposure to negative people. A few years ago, my wife and I were having dinner with another couple. About midway through the evening, I realized this was a very negative night. The couple was gossiping about other people, complaining about the service and food, and bragging about their kids. At one point, I actually told them that their kids made our kids look below average. When the night ended and we were on our way back home, Laura and I simultaneously said, "We are never going out with that couple again." It was a rare night out for us and it was wasted on spending time with negative people. Why would we choose to subject ourselves to such negativity?

Out of some sense of obligation, many of us spend time with negative people. Let me give you some advice. Get rid of the negative people. If you can't, at least try to diminish the influence they have on you and your family. To remain persistently positive, you have to rid your life of negative influences. This task alone could take dogged persistence. Some of you reading this will realize that you yourself might be negative. Don't be discouraged. Just start now by making a conscious effort to stay positive or stay quiet. You have a tremendous impact on others! Take a moment to think about how you influence others and if you should be more careful in your behavior and in your conversations.

POWER OF PERSISTENCE

You want to win in business? Be persistent. Persistence in great customer service earns the repeat customer. Persistent attention to detail achieves excellence. Persistence in the fundamentals of sales helps land the deal. As

You want to win in business? Be persistent.

leaders, persistence in character and behavior shows integrity. In showing persistence in these areas, you have a silent impact on those around you and that impact is profound. Persistence will help you achieve success in athletics or business or life. "Good enough" isn't good enough if you want to be the best.

"MANY PEOPLE SPEND MORE
TIME IN PLANNING THE WEDDING THAN THEY
DO IN PLANNING THE MARRIAGE."

—ZIG ZIGLAR

Zig Ziglar is a legendary thought leader who continues to inspire people with his philosophy, even after his death. Part of being persistent in your preparation is to prepare in a smart manner. Are you preparing for the most magical wedding day ever or are you preparing for a lifetime of happiness and successful communication with your new spouse? I am convinced that everyone works hard or thinks they work hard, but the most successful people work hard and also work with an intelligent plan in place.

THE JOURNEY

As a journalist, you often know the answer before you ask the question. I have done hundreds of stories with former professional athletes and Olympic champions on life when the cheers stop. The standard question to ask is, "What do you miss the most?" The answer is the same 99.9 percent of the time: "I miss my teammates and the camaraderie of the locker room or clubhouse."

One of the next questions in the interview is, "Do you have any regrets?" The cliché answer is that the athlete has no regrets and he or she would not do a thing differently. If that is the answer, I dig a little more because I firmly believe we all have regrets. We all would have handled certain situations differently if we had a second

We don't take time to celebrate the small wins.

chance. When I dig a little deeper and get athletes to open up and really reflect on their careers, here is what many of them will confess: "I wish I would have enjoyed it more while I was playing the game."

There is a lesson in this for all of us. Too many times we get so caught up in the big goal that we don't enjoy the journey. We don't take time to celebrate the small wins and analyze the things we will do differently the next time we face adversity. Part of being an influential person is being intentional. You can influence your future by living intentionally now.

AND THE WINNER IS . . .

The annual high school athletic banquet is probably a bigger deal in a small school than a big school. I went to a small school and I remember my senior banquet quite well. It was your basic rubber chicken dinner followed by every coach getting up and handing out individual awards to the athletes. The Seymour High School Athletic Banquet in 1975 turned into the Joe Schmit Pity Party, and I was the only person invited.

Ever since I can remember, I loved sports and I played sports. Whatever sport was in season, I played it. I had two older brothers and a bunch of neighborhood friends. Together we played some sort of game every night of the summer and whenever we could during the school year. We would choose sides for baseball, hockey, basketball, football, and of course, one of the greatest sports never to become an Olympic sport, kick the can.

From grade school on, I played three sports a year in school. When football season ended, I would join the wrestling team. When that season was over, it was baseball season. Seymour was a small school, so by the time I was a sophomore I was playing on the varsity team in all three sports. I was not a great natural athlete; it was purely a numbers game. I like to say that Seymour High School was so small that we had Driver's Education and Sex Education in the very same car. That's a joke, but I want to make sure everyone understands that no colleges, junior colleges, tech schools, or beer league softball teams were recruiting me as a blue-chip prospect.

My mom and dad were at the awards banquet that night and so were the parents of all my buddies. As the night went on and each coach got up and gave out MVP trophies, All-Conference plaques, and other various individual awards, I started to sink in my chair. It seemed like every single one of my friends was getting up to be honored, but my name was not being called. I thought, *All this work I put in. All the time I spent trying to be a good teammate and all the blood, sweat, and tears was just not worth it.* The only thing missing from my dive into a depressed state was a violin playing in a minor key.

Because I had attended this banquet since I was in seventh grade, I knew that the final award of the night was the Lions Club Scholarship. This went to the top senior student athlete. It was an award voted on by all of the coaches. Most figured the award would be given to one of two seniors who won state track titles. This was before high schools had a class system based on enrollment, so for two kids from a small school like Seymour to win state championships was extremely rare.

When the Lions Club president announced the award, I remember him saying, "For the first time ever, we have two winners." Everyone knew it was going to be the two track athletes. The first name was the state long-jump champion and the second was . . . Joe Schmit. My mom gasped in such loud surprise that people laughed. I stayed low in my chair for an extra pause, feeling guilty for the pity party and feeling shocked that I had been given such an honor!

When they read the coaches' comments on why they voted for me, I began to realize that it is not about the award, but rather the journey I took to get there. One of the coaches said, "Joe is not a naturally gifted athlete, but nobody did more with what they had."

Another coach said, "Every coach would love to have more Joe Schmits on their team. He's very deserving of this honor."

Live by the mouth and die by the mouth, when I went up to accept the award, I decided to grab the microphone. (I know, what a shock!) I stood in front of all the coaches who had voted for me, all my friends and teammates, and their parents and said I didn't deserve the award. I said my buddy, the other state track champ, should be up there. I did not mean to offend anyone, but I guess it was a moment of raw honesty because I knew there were better athletes. That wasn't the only mistake I made in my fumbling speech. I should have thanked my big brothers, Jim and John. The only reason I was a varsity athlete at all was because they pushed me when I was young during all those games we played with the neighborhood kids.

Reporter's NOTEBOOK

I can't tell you how many times I relived that night at the awards banquet. It really hit me that what I learned on the journey was far more important than the trophy I won. Sports taught me that there are no shortcuts in life. I learned how to pay the price, how to win, and more importantly, how to lose. I can still hear some of the wise things my coaches said to me along the way. The friends I had in high school are still my friends today—once a teammate, always a teammate.

> *It really hit me that what I learned on the journey was far more important than the trophy I won.*

The scholarship from the Lions Club was for $500. At that time, I really wanted to go to college but did not know how I could afford it. We had six kids in the family and my parents could only help out minimally. Though the scholarship was not that much money, it propelled me to go for my dream. I became the first member of my family to graduate from college. That pity party may have been the best party I have ever attended!

PURSUIT OF HAPPINESS

The United States Constitution is one of the greatest documents ever written. Our forefathers set the stage in the late 1700s for the freedoms we now enjoy. In this document, citizens of the United States are guaranteed certain unalienable rights: "Life, liberty, and the pursuit of happiness." The US of A is not perfect, but we do value life and have the kinds of liberties that many other countries do not enjoy. Where we fail many times as Americans is in our pursuit of happiness.

Happiness is a choice. Happiness is contagious. People of influence know this and spread their happiness like Tinker Bell sprinkles her pixie dust. Every morning when you get out of bed, you can choose to have a positive attitude or a negative attitude. You can't choose the weather and you can't control what happens in the world, but you can decide how you will approach each day. Control is an illusion. You can only control your actions and your reactions. Try this exercise. Before you get out of bed in the morning, think of all the great things in your life. Make a list of them and then pledge to yourself that you are going to have a great day looking forward to the challenges that are ahead of you.

I believe the easiest way to become a happier person is to become a more generous person. Go and volunteer. Do something good for the community and yourself. I have met many of my closest friends through charity work. I have yet to meet a miserable person who gives of themselves.

In today's celebrity culture, some people think they can find happiness through fame and fortune. We live in an age where reality TV and social media make people famous for being famous. The truth is, money does not buy happiness. I think about the final scene of Frank Capra's classic movie *It's a Wonderful Life* where George Bailey is a very frustrated banker who wishes he was never born. By the end of the movie, George realizes that he has had a positive impact on many people in the community. His brother Harry, a war hero, returns home on Christmas Eve and salutes his brother, "Here's to George Bailey, the richest man in town." Character, integrity, and generosity don't always show up in your bank account, but they do in your overall happiness and well-being.

> *I have yet to meet a miserable person who gives of themselves.*

PASSION

THE WINNER'S CIRCLE

I have been lucky enough in my career to conduct one-on-one interviews with some of the biggest names in sports, including Muhammad Ali, Tiger Woods, Michael Jordan, Jack Nicklaus, Adrian Peterson, and Wayne Gretzky. I tried to analyze what they all have in common. First of all, they are all rich and incredibly talented athletes. But what they really have in common is passion. They have the passion to be the best, which means they have the passion to compete and the passion to prepare to compete. As a result of their passion, they have amplified their influence. They are true impact players who make everyone around them better just by being themselves.

I covered a boxer in Minnesota by the name of Scott Ledoux. He stepped in the ring with eight world heavyweight-boxing champions. He lost all eight fights. They called him "the Great White Hope" and he said it worked for him because he was white and he was hoping. Ledoux's best fight was against George Foreman when he was the world heavyweight champion. Now this was before George Foreman invented the George Foreman Grill and ate a whole bunch of cheeseburgers off the grill. When Foreman stepped into the ring with Ledoux, he was a lean, mean, fighting machine.

For eight rounds, Scott Ledoux went toe-to-toe with Foreman until the champ poked Ledoux in the eye with his thumb. Ledoux's eye swelled shut and he couldn't see, so the referee called the fight. Ledoux's dream ended with a technical knockout. Later in the locker room, a doctor examined his eye and said, "Scott, I'm afraid you are going to lose that eye."

To which Ledoux responded, "What's an eye when you've given your heart?" Giving your heart the way Scott Ledoux did is pure passion. Never be afraid to show your passion.

THE IMMORTAL WORDS OF MARVIN GAYE

It was maybe the best World Series ever. I know that is saying a lot, but when the Minnesota Twins and the Atlanta Braves battled for the world championship in 1991, it was better drama than any reality TV show.

The Twins trailed the best-of-seven series, three games to two heading into the crucial game six at the Hubert H. Humphrey Metrodome. The place had so much energy that Ben Franklin would not have needed a kite and a key to discover electricity that night. Most people who saw the game will remember the fantastic catch Minnesota Twins center-fielder Kirby Puckett made against the Plexiglas wall in the third inning and his game-winning home run in the bottom of the eleventh inning that forced a game seven. When Puckett hit the home run, the legendary broadcaster Jack Buck made the classic call, "And we will see you tomorrow night." These great moments are not what I remember most. My most vivid memory of that night is something that happened after the game.

Major League Baseball called a news conference after midnight so the two starting pitchers in the seventh and deciding game could answer questions from the media. Deep in the bowels of the Metrodome in Minneapolis, Twins pitcher Jack Morris stepped up to the microphone and said, "In the immortal words of Marvin Gaye, 'Let's get it on.'" I leaned over to the person sitting next to me and said, "The Twins are going to win the World Series." Jack Morris was a passionate competitor and his words made a believer out of me.

"In the immortal words of Marvin Gaye, 'Let's get it on.'"

The next night, Morris went out and pitched arguably one of the best games ever pitched in the World Series. He pitched a ten-inning shutout and the Twins beat the Braves one to nothing for the World Series title. The dome was so loud that my ears were still ringing days later.

Reporter's NOTEBOOK

Jack Morris was a gritty, tough, and sometimes nasty competitor. After pitching nine innings of amazing baseball during that famous game seven of the World Series, Twins manager, Tom

Kelly, and pitching coach, Dick Such, decided that Morris had done all he could do. It was time to put in another pitcher. Kelly approached Morris, who had already thrown 118 pitches. Kelly said, "That's all. Can't ask you to do any more than that." Morris resisted, Kelly argued and then walked away saying to himself, "Ok, it's just a game, so what the hell."

As you know, Morris got the final three outs—the last one a strike out—and the Twins had their second world title in five years. Morris was later quoted saying he was willing to pitch 120 innings. Whenever I hear the classic song by the legendary Marvin Gaye, it takes me back to that early October morning before Jack Morris took the microphone and said, "Let's get it on."

SISTER HELEN

Sister Helen, a Catholic nun from west central Minnesota, originally wrote about this personal story for a small religious, biannual publication called *Proteus, A Journal of Ideas* in 1991. It appeared in *Reader's Digest* in 1991 as well as *Chicken Soup for the Soul* by

Jack Canfield and Mark Victor Hanson in 1993. After that, hundreds of websites and blogs picked up on the inspiring story. I found myself wanting to dig even deeper into Sister Helen's profound example of silent impact. When you read about the influence one small-town nun had on generations of people, you will realize the potential you have for making a difference in the lives of others.

Her full name was Sister Helen (Mary Carmela) Mrolsa. She was born on October 24, 1935, and became a nun in August 1958. She got her master's degree and was a teacher in Minnesota, Texas, and Kentucky. Unfortunately, I found her obituary in the *Brainerd Dispatch* archives; she passed away at the age of sixty-four at St. Francis Convent in Little Falls, Minnesota. The obituary had all the rudimentary facts about her life, but it was missing something significant. It did not tell about the silent impact Sister Helen had made on her students and families.

Sister Helen was a third-grade teacher at St. Mary's Catholic School in Morris, a small farming community in west central Minnesota. She had a student by the name of Mark Ecklund. Sister Helen noticed a special energy and charisma in Mark. He was a little bit of a troublemaker who talked too much, yet had a "happy-to-be-alive attitude." One time she put masking tape over Mark's mouth to get him to stop talking. Needless to say, it did not work.

Several years later, Sister Helen was teaching ninth-grade math in the same school district. She discovered a familiar name on her class roster—Mark Ecklund. He had grown in height and handsomeness, but he still had a big personality with a propensity to get in trouble. One week, Sister Helen was trying to teach the class a new math concept, but the class was just not getting it. The students became frustrated and they disengaged. That caused Sister Helen to become frustrated because the students were no longer trying to understand.

The veteran teacher knew she had to change the atmosphere in the classroom, so she asked everyone to take out a piece of paper. The kids immediately thought, *Oh no, a pop quiz!* But that was not the case. She instructed everyone to write down all their class-mates' names. Next to each name, they were to write the nicest thing they could say about that person. The classroom got very quiet as the thirty-four students spent the rest of the hour doing this very unconventional assignment.

Sister Helen compiled a list of the compliments for each one of her students. She handed them out to the class on Monday and noticed an immediate change in the aura of the classroom. The students were beaming. She went back to teaching, and soon everybody understood. The exercise accomplished what she was hoping for, and the list wasn't mentioned again all school year.

Several years later, Sister Helen was coming back from vacation. When her parents picked her up at the airport, her dad told her that the Ecklunds had called. And Sister Helen said, "Oh, how is Mark? I have been thinking about him a lot lately." Her dad then broke the news that Mark died while in the Vietnam War and his funeral was the next day. The family wanted Sister Helen to come to the funeral.

Sister Helen was feeling both shocked and saddened as she went to the funeral. It was a cloudy, gray day. Mark was given the full military funeral that a hero deserves. The casket was draped with the red, white, and blue; the choir sang the "Battle Hymn of the Republic"; and a twenty-one-gun salute was given as a bugler played the old familiar "Taps."

Back at Mark's family farm for lunch, his parents approached Sister Helen and told her that the government had sent Mark's belongings back. They had something to show her. They brought her Mark's wallet, opened it up, and pulled out a tattered piece of paper. It had even been carefully repaired with a piece of tape. It was the list. Mark had carried it with him to his dying day.

Soon some of Mark's classmates gathered around and one said, "I still have my list, too. My wife put it in our wedding album." Another said, "I keep mine in my diary." Another took out his wallet and pulled his tattered, crinkled list to show everyone. Remarkable. They had all kept and treasured their list of admired traits.

Reporter's NOTEBOOK

Over four decades later, the lists created on a frustrating day in ninth-grade math class live on. I was able to find and speak to six of Mark's classmates. All six have memorized some of the compliments on their lists. Judy Swanson shared with me that someone liked her smile someone said she was always positive, and someone else said she had nice legs! Judy Swanson says this about the list: "It shaped me."

Vicky McNally said her compliments covered her good posture, her good block letters, and her nice lips. Obviously, hormones were raging for at least one of the boys in Sister Helen's class! They were compliments nonetheless.

The kids in that class had a twentieth class reunion with Sister Helen and almost everyone showed up. "It wasn't surprising because she was treasured by all of us," said Vicky McNally. Bob Johnson was blunt when he described going to a Catholic grade school in the late sixties. He said, "All the nuns looked like Doberman pinschers, but Sister Helen was an angel!"

Chuck Lesmeister was Mark Ecklund's best friend. He admitted that he and Mark were not angels while they were in school. I asked Chuck why he thought Mark carried that list with him to Vietnam. He said if he had to guess, it was because Mark was from a large family and wasn't the type of guy who would receive many compliments during that time of his life. Even though the assignment was mandatory, Mark found significant encouragement and comfort in carrying these words in his pocket half a world away.

Besides the list, Mark's best friend Chuck has something else that he saved. The night before Mark headed off to Vietnam, they drank a couple of beers together. For whatever reason, Chuck kept one of those beer cans as a sign of sharing many more in the years to come. Today that beer can rests on the mantle of Chuck's fireplace. It is a silent tribute to his friend who will always be in his heart.

Jim Halbe missed Mark Ecklund's funeral. He had a very legitimate excuse, after all. Jim was still fighting in the war in Vietnam. In his wallet was . . . the list. I asked him why he carried it. He said, "It was a security blanket for bad days."

A common theme in speaking to these former students is that they tried to pass on Sister Helen's lessons to their children and grandchildren. The message was simple but significant: You can always find something positive to say about someone. Praise more, condemn less.

Reporter's NOTEBOOK II

What Sister Helen did was live with passion. When you care passionately, you make a lasting impact on others. As we've seen with Sister Helen, your impact can be contagious. It's real, it's prolific, and it can last for years.

Sister Helen was not afraid to show her passion for the kids in her classroom. She realized the secret to being a person of influence: It's not about them feeling good about you. It's about them feeling good about themselves. That's how you become an impact player. That's how you make everyone around you better. Silent impact proves that self-esteem is not just an issue for teenagers. One of the most powerful ways to make an impact is to lift someone's self-esteem.

> *She realized the secret to being a person of influence: It's not about them feeling good about you. It's about them feeling good about themselves.*

Mark's friend Jim called the list a "security blanket." We all need that security blanket every now and then. If you want to have a true impact on someone's life, be aware of the people around you. Someone might need you to show that you care. Just like Sister Helen, you can make a silent impact.

SMILE

New York Times best-selling author Harvey Mackay says in his book *Swim with the Sharks* that the most important hiring decision a company makes is for the receptionist position. Receptionists are a company's first impression. They are the people who greet visitors and patrons and they often answer the phone as well. A good first impression is essential!

How many times are you on the phone and you can tell the person on the other end of the line is smiling and filled with energy? You are drawn to that person like a magnet. Try it yourself for a week. Smile when you are on the phone. See if it helps you make a better connection with the person on the other end.

The same thing can be said of the voice message you leave on your phone. If you sound bored and uninterested, that is the tone you will set. I always end my message with, "Have a terrific day." I mean it and many times people will repeat it back to me when they leave their message. A positive attitude is contagious and makes a positive impact.

DRIVE-THRU SERVICE

I recently spoke to a large group from Wendy's Restaurants. The group included franchise owners, district managers, and general managers from stores in the Midwest. As a matter of fact, this was such an important meeting that Wendy Thomas herself was there. She is the girl on the iconic Wendy's logo who the restaurant was named after.

After I delivered my keynote on *Silent Impact: Stories of Influence through Purpose, Persistence, and Passion*, one of the people in the audience came up to tell me a personal story that illustrated my topic. This is a normal occurrence after my presentations because many people have their own story of silent impact that they want to share.

The lady told me that at one of their Wendy's restaurants, an elderly gentleman would come daily and order breakfast from the drive-thru window. It was like clockwork; the old Buick would pull up and order the same food every morning at seven thirty. During the week, the same employee would welcome him to Wendy's, take his order, and complete the transaction. Every morning, this Wendy's team member would greet the old man with a big, friendly smile, ask him how he was doing that day, and sincerely wish him a good day as he drove away.

One day, the man did not order his food through the drive thru. He entered the restaurant and asked for the young lady who had been serving him breakfast for the past couple of months. He told her that he wanted to hug her and thank her.

The server was somewhat surprised, but she hugged the man. He said, "Every morning when I stop by for breakfast, I am on my way to the nursing home to visit my wife, who is in hospice. She passed away last night so I won't be stopping by so often anymore." The young lady did not know what to say, so she hugged him again. The old man said that stopping at Wendy's every morning was the highlight of his day. "You will never know how much your smile and friendly attitude meant to me. That's the way my wife saw the world until she got sick."

SILENT IMPACT

It's the little things in life that really are the big things. A smile, a friendly attitude, and a heart of gratitude can have an impact on the world.

Reporter's NOTEBOOK

When Dave Thomas started Wendy's in November 1969, his first and foremost goal was to serve great hamburgers. His motto then is still preached today, "Quality is our recipe." While he was serving great hamburgers and building the Wendy's empire, he also decided that he wanted to give back to the communities he served.

That is when he started the Dave Thomas Foundation for Adoption that has helped more than 3,500 children get adopted from foster care. Dave Thomas himself was adopted, but his adoptive mother died when he was five. Passionate about orphans and the adoptive families who love them, Dave Thomas used his fame and platform to make a lasting impact in this area of adoption. Talk about an impact player.

EVERYONE NEEDS A BUD

When Bud Lindberg was seven years old, he was climbing a tree on his family farm in rural Wisconsin to get a bird's nest to show his little brother. He grabbed a power line and lost three fingers on his left hand and had limited use of his right hand. The childhood accident was devastating, but Bud did not let it define him.

A year after Bud lost his fingers in the accident, his father died of a heart attack. The family was poverty stricken, but Bud was able to overcome his physical and financial limitations to go to college and then seminary to become a Lutheran minister. Bud not only played high school sports, but also amazed everyone by playing college football at Gustavus Adolphus College in St. Peter, Minnesota.

Bud was one of the pastors at my family's church, Mt. Olivet Lutheran Church in Minneapolis, Minnesota. Churchgoers were always greeted with a huge smile and an even bigger hug. If Bud felt he knew you well enough, he would use the one finger he had left on his left hand and stick it in your ear. It was his unique way of making you smile and letting you know he cared. Bud passed away in November 2008 at the age of eighty-five. Up until the end, he remained very active in the church, still giving hugs and silly finger pokes.

In 2012, Craig Johnson, senior pastor of Mt. Olivet Lutheran Church, was giving the sermon on generosity when he started talking about his hero, Laurel "Bud" Lindberg. He told the story of how Bud grew up with bare cupboards and one finger on his left hand. Then he told this story.

A nurse from Children's Hospital in Minneapolis called Pastor Lindberg and told him about a little boy who had just suffered a similar hand injury to Bud's childhood injury. The boy was extremely distraught at his loss and deeply struggling. She asked Bud if he could come down and talk with the boy. Bud accepted. As Bud began his conversation with the boy, the boy asked him, "Can you still write?" (*Yes*) "Can you tie your shoes?" (*Yes*) "Can you brush your teeth?" (*Yes*) The little boy loved basketball the most of all. "Can you shoot a basket?" Bud swallowed hard and answered, "Yes."

"Then show me," said the boy. There was a small gym in the basement of the church, so that is where Bud and the boy headed. Bud was anything but a basketball player. The whole way to the little gym, Pastor Lindberg prayed his heart out. *Dear God, help me to make my first basket in thirty years!* He got the ball, took aim from fifteen feet and . . . *swish*. The little boy was overwhelmed with feelings of relief and happiness. And then he said, "Do it again!"

Reporter's NOTEBOOK

Jeanne Wyatt was the nurse who called Pastor Lindberg that day and I was able to talk to her about her recollections. "The young boy was just so depressed. I just felt so sorry for the boy and his mother that I wanted to help out. Bud's situation came to my mind, so I made the call." Nurse Jeanne recalls that Pastor Lindberg met with the boy on Good Friday, one of the holiest and busiest days of the year at Mt. Olivet. She was impressed that he made time to meet with young boy. Pastor Lindberg admitted later that he was as nervous as ever when he shot that basketball. One could argue it was a moment of divine impact!

JIMMY V

Jim "Jimmy V" Valvano is the late, great basketball coach of North Carolina State. He led the Wolfpack to a surprising NCAA title in 1983. The video of Coach Valvano running around on the court looking for someone to hug after winning the title game is replayed every single year during March Madness. But as much success as Jimmy V had on the basketball court, it does not compare to the impact he had off the court. The ripple effects of his impact continue to this day, even though he passed away in 1993.

Valvano was diagnosed with an aggressive, inoperable cancer in June 1992. The prognosis was bad. ESPN, where Valvano worked, was airing an awards show, and they planned to honor Valvano at the event. ESPN also announced the formation of the Jimmy V Foundation for Cancer Research.

At the banquet, Valvano was so weak he needed help to climb up five stairs to get to the stage. When he stepped in front of the microphone, his cancer took a backseat to his passion. He gave one of the great speeches ever recorded when he pleaded with the audience, "Don't give up, don't ever give up."

But what he also talked about in that presentation was the definition of a perfect day. He said a perfect day was one in which you laughed, you cried, and you had time to think. The human being is the only creature on God's earth with the ability to laugh. Your perfect day should include laughter. Valvano also said that you should get so moved by something that you are

> . . . *A perfect day was one in which you laughed, you cried, and you had time to think.*

moved to tears. And finally, you think deeply about something and maybe break new ground. You look at something from a different angle and you have an epiphany. The elements of a perfect day are similar to the elements of the best movies of all times. They make us laugh, move us to tears, and cause us to think. When was the last time you had a perfect day according to Valvano's definition? What are you going to do tomorrow to ensure that you have a perfect day? If you live your life with passion, you will have plenty of perfect days. As Jimmy V said himself, "You do that seven days a week, you're going to have something special."

Reporter's NOTEBOOK

I recently spent some time with Dick Vitale from ESPN. He was one of Valvano's best friends and has worked tirelessly to raise money and awareness for the V Foundation. That foundation has now raised an amazing $100 million for cancer research. I asked Dick what he thought Jim Valvano would say today if he could see what has happened with the charity named in his honor. As only Dickie V could say, "How do you know he's not watching right now, baby?" He went on to remember what Jimmy V said in the speech: "Don't give up, don't ever give up." The money raised for the foundation did not come in time to help him, but it will help generations to come.

THE BRIDGE TO CARING

One of the best pieces of advice I received when I began speaking on a more regular basis was to show the audience my heart. You can connect with people in a very personal way when you are authentic, empathetic, and vulnerable. I have experienced this to be true on stage and admire these qualities in Sona Mehring, the founder of CaringBridge.org.

In 1997, a close friend of Sona Mehring's had a premature baby who had serious medical complications. When baby Bridhid was born, her parents asked Sona to let the many friends and family members concerned know what was going on. Sona decided to create a website to allow family members to communicate information to a wide network of concerned people. They posted daily journal entries and allowed visitors to send the family messages of love and encouragement. The response was incredible, and Sona knew what she had to do. Sadly, Bridhid only lived a few days, but the wave of love for that little girl and her family live on through a website that became the gold standard for the strength of the human spirit.

Sona Mehring was running a successful consulting business at the time, but after seeing the power of the site for Bridhid, she had a new calling. She understood that people want to be there for their friends and loved ones in times of crisis, but they don't always know how to show their care and concern. CaringBridge quickly became the leading social health network in the world. The website and the company grew organically. People would recommend it to others who have used it. The ripple effect was something every business dreams about. CaringBridge was a valuable solution to the communication gap that comes when someone is dealing with a medical crisis and doesn't have the time or energy to update everyone individually. It is more private than Facebook and creates a sense of community among those who read and post journal entries.

Sona Mehring received her first donation, a one hundred-dollar check from a grandmother in California, who was able to stay connected while her grandchild in Minnesota who was going through a medical crisis. The emotional impact the site was having on people was profound. CaringBridge users would find that writing about their journey was in itself therapeutic. The love from others offered hope and a tangible record of their support. The personal stories inspired and motivated people to come together.

Reporter's **NOTEBOOK**

Sona Mehring saw the potential in CaringBridge right away, but she did not think she would be working there seventeen years later. In my interview with Sona she said, "It wasn't my dream, but it became my destiny. It was the path I was supposed to follow."

Sona admitted that her first instinct was to make the website a for-profit venture. After all, she

> *It wasn't my dream, but it became my destiny. It was the path I was supposed to follow.*

was an entrepreneur at heart. She funded the first five years of the project out of her own pocket and then became a 501(c)3 charity in 2002. Sona realized that CaringBridge needed to be community driven.

In 2012, 46 million people visited CaringBridge.org. There have been more than 400,000 personal sites created since 1997. On an average day, over 500,000 people visit the site. Over 2 billion visits have been logged since its inception. Sona was the lone employee in 1997. Today, CaringBridge has sixty-seven employees, a governing board of fourteen members, and more than 1,200 volunteers. Nearly 90 percent of all funding comes from donations from individuals and families who use CaringBridge.

Once a month, Sona invites a family to the company headquarters to speak to the staff about the impact they made on the life of a family. It's always an emotional time as the staff gets to see firsthand the silent impact their work has made on an individual family. It motivates them to continue their great work at CaringBridge.

Sona Mehring has written a book that features personal stories of the magic of CaringBridge called *Hope Conquers All*. Sona is an example to us all that things we do for ourselves die, but things we do for others live on and on. CaringBridge not only became Sona's destiny; it became her legacy.

USE YOUR CIRCLE OF INFLUENCE

Passion can be powerful and it can be contagious. Mark Zuckerberg is the young genius who cofounded Facebook. Before Zuckerberg and his wife, Priscilla Chan, were married, Priscilla worked her way through medical school. During this time, she worked in the transplant unit of a hospital. Zuckerberg enjoyed hearing her joyful stories of patients being matched with donors and felt her sadness when others would run out of time. Zuckerberg thought, *What can I do to help this situation?* Owner of the number-one social network in the world, Zuckerberg directed his staff to start a campaign to entice people to sign up to become organ donors. In the first day of the project, 100,000 people had signed up. By the end of the first week, over 1 million people had registered to be donors!

Because Zuckerberg was aware of the impact organ donors could have on his fiancée and everyone involved, he was inspired to help out. Just imagine how many people whose lives will be changed because of this in the future. We all don't run social networks and the oodles of wealth that comes with that scene, but we do have significant influence on people in our own network of friends, family, coworkers, and neighbors.

Yes, a CEO of a major public company can make an influence, but what about a lower-ranking employee who is just trying to make ends meet? Chances are you have never heard the name Joey Prusak, but you may have heard about his story.

Joey was working at Dairy Queen on Main Street in Hopkins, Minnesota. He was working behind the counter when he noticed a woman pick up a twenty-dollar bill that was just dropped by a visually impaired man who was a regular customer and had just placed his order. When the woman stepped up to the counter to place her order, nineteen-year-old Joey said, "Please return the twenty-dollar bill to the gentleman." When she said it was her money, Joey refused to serve her. The woman was livid, swore repeatedly at Joey, and eventually stormed out of the Dairy Queen.

Here's where Joey took a step that made him an impact player. He took twenty dollars out of his own pocket and gave it to the man who was enjoying his ice cream sundae, unaware of what had just transpired. A Dairy Queen customer who observed this entire scene was so moved that she sent a detailed e-mail to the Dairy Queen corporate headquarters. The story came back to the owner of Joey's Dairy Queen and the story was proudly posted in the restaurant.

In today's age of social media, good deeds can spread like wildfire. Soon, major media outlets picked up the story and Joey Prusak was flooded with requests for interviews. Joey even got a phone call from Warren Buffet, who is the president, chairman, and CEO of Dairy Queen's parent company. Buffet invited Joey to the Berkshire Hathaway shareholders meeting in May 2014 in Omaha, Nebraska.

How many people did Joey Prusak inspire to make an impact? It's hard to say, but his circle of influence grew to enormity very quickly. We have seen that good deeds can be contagious. For example, many people are now paying for the food ordered by the people in the car behind them in the drive thru. Many radio stations have caught on to this movement and have helped propel this idea named the "Drive Thru Difference."

Many times you will see someone pick up the tab at a restaurant where they see military personnel having a meal. I was having lunch with my friend Ron Maddox, who ran a major festival in Minnesota each summer called the Taste of Minnesota. He was a big guy with a big heart. As we walked into the restaurant, we greeted three soldiers who were dressed in their fatigues.

We had lunch and as the bill came, Ron, who was sitting with his back to the soldiers, said, "Joe, you pick up this tab, I will get those guys in the military back there." I chuckled and said sure. What Ron did not realize was that during our lunch, the table of soldiers had grown to about a dozen! He turned around and said, "Oh shoot," or something close to that. Ron took it in stride, though you might want to do a head count before you commit to paying for a group's bill!

Ron had another silent impact on me. During the Taste of Minnesota, Ron would ride around the vast festival grounds on his golf cart to make sure everything was running smoothly. Every time he saw a person in a wheelchair, he would stop to greet them, make sure their experience was satisfactory, and give them ten-dollars-worth of food tickets. I asked him why he did it and he said, "I figure that they had to really make an extra effort to get here and I want to make sure they are recognized for it." Ron passed away recently, but I still fondly remember his generosity and the impact he had on me.

There are boundless opportunities to show kindness and generosity. Live awake, be aware, and always care.

WHAT'S YOUR TRIGGER?

On January 17, 1999, the Minnesota Vikings were about to return to the Super Bowl for the first time in twenty-two years. The Vikings had cruised through the regular season with a 15–1 record and pretty much everyone agreed they were the best team in the NFL. However, a funny thing happened on the way to the Super Bowl. The Vikings lost in the NFC Championship Game to the Atlanta Falcons.

This was a gut-wrenching loss for the Minnesota Vikings franchise and their hard-luck fans. Not only did the Vikings lose their chance to return to the Super Bowl, but they also lost the game at the Metrodome, their home field, in front of their loyal and expectant fans.

Cris Carter had been one of the best receivers in the NFL for a decade. He knew he was getting close to the end of his career and also knew that he would not have many more chances of playing in the Super Bowl. Number 80, Cris Carter, caught my eye after the game ended. He stood motionless near the goal line, watching the Atlanta Falcons players' euphoria as they celebrated their upset, reaching the pinnacle of their profession.

The next summer when the Vikings reported for training camp, the start of their journey that they hoped would end in the next Super Bowl, I asked Carter about watching the Falcons celebrate. "Why did you do it?" I asked Carter. He replied, "I wanted to remember the pain. Whenever I was working out in the off-season and wanted to quit, I would remember the pain and I would not quit."

What's your trigger? What can you say to yourself to push you to be the best? We all need to be motivated, and sometimes the biggest influence can come from deep within. I believe in the power of these personal pep talks. We all need a pat on the back or a kick in the rear every now and then.

Reporter's NOTEBOOK

Cris Carter never did play in a Super Bowl, but he did accomplish something pretty special. He was voted into the Pro Football Hall of Fame in 2013. Carter's off-season workouts were legendary. Sometimes he had to remember the pain to push himself so later he could enjoy the rewards.

I must share one more story about Cris Carter. The Vikings had another outstanding receiver by the name of Anthony Carter. One day after practice, Cris Carter was helping a rookie receiver by teaching him some of the finer points of catching the football. Anthony Carter saw what Cris was doing and said, "Why are you helping that rookie? Someday he's going to take your job." To which Cris responded, "Someday he is going to help us win a game!"

Which Carter are you? What kind of a teammate are you? An impact player always puts the team first, no exceptions.

THE SECOND THANK YOU

Chances are the mere mention of high school conjures up a complex array of emotions. For many of us, it was a tremendous time of creating memories, forming friendships, and learning valuable life lessons. Except for a few bumps in the road, most feel as though our high school experiences helped shape our interests and played a key role in the person we are today.

For some, high school was pure horror, something to endure. The suffering was often silent, but the damage always devastating. Meet Sam and Kristin.

Sam Richter was a star athlete in high school who eventually played NCAA Division I football. Sam won many medals and trophies during this time of his life, but his most significant contribution had nothing to do with his athletic prowess.

Kristin was a freshman at Sam's high school. She was being routinely bullied by a boy in the school. She was struggling with confidence and wondering why teachers kept looking the other way when the bullying would take place in the hallways. That's not all. Kristin's grandmother, to whom she was close, had just passed away. And her father, who had been absent from her life, had just left the family for good.

One day Kristin was being bullied in the hallway again. Sam did not know Kristin, but when he walked by the bullying incident, he was disturbed. Sam stepped into the situation and told the boy, "Back off! And if you ever try this again, you will have to deal with me!" Then in a moment of both maturity and sensitivity, he turned to Kristin and said, "If he ever bothers you again, let me know!"

Twenty-three years after graduating from high school, Sam received an e-mail from Kristin. The name rang a bell, but Sam had forgotten all about the incident:

Hi Sam,

You probably don't remember me, but I sure remember you. You were a senior and a star on the football team while I was an insecure, unpopular freshman. One day I was standing by my locker and a kid was bullying me. But it wasn't just any kid. I was scared of this kid because he had bullied me many times before. You came over and told him to knock it off, and if he wanted to be mean to anyone, he would have to go through you. You told me that if he ever picked on me again, to come look you up. What you didn't realize is that I was at the lowest point in my life that day. I was going to go home, take a bunch of sleeping pills, and hope to never wake up. I was ready to do anything to stop the pain. You saved my life that day. And I just wanted to thank you.

—Kristin

This is how silent impact works. We make our biggest impressions when we are not trying to be impressive.

Reporter's NOTEBOOK

Today, Kristin is a successful radio personality in the Midwest. One day, a news release crossed her desk that contained the name Sam Richter. Kristin did a little research and realized that this was the same Sam Richter from high school. There was no doubt in her mind what she had to do. She wrote the e-mail to let Sam know about the impact he had on her from that poignant moment in high school. It was a scene that lasted no more than ninety seconds, but one she had played out in her mind many times since then. She could remember what she was wearing that day, the color of the walls, and the number on her locker. It was a moment that changed the arc of Kristin's life.

Sam had no idea what Kristin was going through twenty-three years earlier. He simply acted instinctively, wanting to do the right thing. "Sam made me feel like I wasn't alone anymore," Kristin said when I interviewed her. "He was exactly where he was supposed to be. He stood up for me!"

Kristin reached out to Sam because she felt he deserved to know that he was her hero. She worked her way through school as a cashier at a grocery store and wondered what she would say if Sam happened to come into her store. While reading the book *The Five People You Meet in Heaven* by Mitch Albom, she was certain that Sam would be one of those five people. Needless to say, the e-mail from Kristin was a treasure to Sam.

Is there someone in your life you could thank for the impact they have had on you?

What Kristin did is what I call the Second Thank You. It is going back to someone who had a silent impact on you and letting him or her know what that meant to you. Is there someone in your life you could thank for the impact they have had on you? Do it! You will make their day . . . heck you may make their whole year! You never know what kind of impact your second thank you might have on *them*. If that person of influence is no longer on earth, find one of their children or family members. The impact will be immediate and real.

SHARE YOUR STORY

Is there someone whom you would like to thank for having a major impact on your life? I would love to hear your story! I believe we can start a movement of gratitude. Who knows, I may include your story in my next book.

On May 14, 2013, the thirtieth anniversary of my dad's death, someone started a Facebook post with a picture of my dad. Soon, all kinds of friends, cousins, and people I did not even know started writing wonderful tributes about my dad. Guess what—it made my day, and yes, I still feel good when I think about that online expression of gratitude over the impact my dad made on others.

Let me hear your stories.
Write me at **joe@joeschmit.com**.

THE UNION

Elton John understands the value and power of the second thank you. The legendary singer and songwriter's career took off like a "Rocket Man" when he arrived on the American music scene in 1970. Elton John said his musical idol at the time was Leon Russell. The two met at John's second show ever in the United States; they became friends and made great music together for a short period of time.

Many years later, Elton was traveling with his partner, David Furnish, in Africa when David started to play some old songs from Leon Russell off his iPod. Elton recognized the voice and merger of soul and gospel only Russell could do. It was at that moment he knew he had to reconnect with the man who meant so much to him earlier in his career.

Feeling compelled to reach out and reconnect to his idol, Elton John called Russell and asked him if he was interested in writing an album together. It was 2009 and at that time, Russell was an aging, all but burned-out rocker who was making ends meet playing small-time gigs. Here was a man who had previously collaborated on records with Frank Sinatra, Jerry Lee Lewis, the Beach Boys, Joe Cocker, and the Rolling

Stones. Russell used to perform in front of twenty thousand people on a regular basis. Now, his career had dwindled down to audiences of a few hundred.

Leon Russell was not a charity case for Elton John. John recognized the musical genius in Russell and wanted to collaborate to create something special. It was also a way to say thank you for being there for a young, flamboyant, emerging singer and songwriter from England decades ago.

The Union was released in 2010 and peaked at number three on the United States record charts. It was Elton John's thirtieth album and Leon Russell's first hit since 1979. A behind-the-scenes documentary produced by filmmaker Cameron Crowe during the creative process has garnered critical acclaim.

Reporter's NOTEBOOK

Elton John and Leon Russell had not spoken in thirty-eight years, yet because Elton made the effort to go back and thank someone who influenced his career, it revived Russell's life and career also. One year after *The Union* was released, Leon Russell was elected into the Rock and Roll Hall of Fame. As you might expect, Elton John was his presenter. In his eloquent speech, John said, "He sang, he wrote, and he played like I wanted to do."

At the ceremony, Russell said, "Elton found me in the ditch by the side of the highway of life. He took me up to the high stages with big audiences and treated me like a king." Russell finished his acceptance speech with this emotional finish. "Bless your heart. Hallelujah!"

FRIENDS IN LOW PLACES

Having sold more albums than the Beatles, I think it's safe to call Garth Brooks a legend. He has sold almost 70 million albums and is in the Country Music Hall of Fame. "Friends in Low Places," one of his most famous songs, took on a whole new meaning for me after I heard a story about Garth from a security guard who had recently worked one of his concerts at the Target Center in Minneapolis. You see, Garth took care of some people in "high places" . . . people sitting in the rafters of the building.

The security guard told me that Garth left the two rows directly in front of the stage open for his concert. Before he took the stage, Garth sent some of his crew out into the arena to look for fans sitting in the worst seats in the house—those sitting in the top row or those with obstructed views—and invite them to enjoy the concert from the best seats in the house!

Later, I was part of a charity event in which Garth performed, so I took the opportunity to ask him about this unique tradition of inviting the folks in the cheapest seats to move to the front. He said, "I do it because I figure that anyone who paid their hard-earned money to sit in lousy seats to hear me in concert is a big fan, and I want to give them the best experience possible." Garth said he wanted his most enthusiastic fans in the front, not people who had thick enough wallets to buy tickets at crazy prices.

You don't survive and thrive in a tough business like the music industry without "getting it." A small gesture by a giant in country music shows that expressing loyalty and gratitude can have a profound impact.

INFLUENTIAL LEADERSHIP

If you have employees who are engaged in the culture of your company, you have worked to understand what and who influences them. The employees who would garner the biggest crowd at their going-away party are the people who are invaluable to your organization. As leaders, we need to recognize their powerful influence and do what we can to foster their greatness.

According to Don MacPherson, president of Modern Survey, in March 2013 employees are unhappy and disengaged at record levels. Employee disengagement among one thousand surveyed US workers, according to the semiannual National Employee Engagement Study, is at 32 percent. An additional 22 percent of those surveyed are "somewhat" into their jobs. In other words, over half of those employed right now don't like their jobs nor do they feel ownership in the company's culture and bottom line. If these numbers don't scare you, I am not sure what will!

Guess which half of the employee spectrum holds the influential people? You know who they are. They are not the whiners, they are the givers. They are vested in the success of your company. They take the three Ps to their job everyday: Purpose, Persistence, and Passion.

Leaders need to be smart enough to understand their power of influence. Believe it or not, more people leave their jobs because they feel underappreciated than because they feel underpaid. My speaker friend Mike McKinley always says, "I never heard of anyone who quit his or her job because they were sick of people telling them how good of a job they were doing." Mike jokes during his presentations saying, "Every time I turn around, somebody is patting me on the back and telling me how good of a job I am doing. I cannot stand it anymore."

The worst bosses are the "gotcha" bosses—the ones who are right there to point out your mistakes or criticize you for something that didn't go quite right. Influential leaders are "gotcha" bosses too, except they spend their energy pointing out the positives in their employee's performance. Too many times, people wait until the big project is over to throw out the compliments. You might be surprised how much a few well-placed positive "gotchas" will help keep your team happy and motivated.

> The worst bosses are the "gotcha" bosses.

Many companies use the words *team* and *team members* when they talk about their staff, but please avoid using those terms as cliché. Make everyone on the team, no matter what their role, feel important. Gratitude can be contagious.

In most research and publications on the power of influence, the word *persuasion* is used. I have purposely avoided that word because I believe the strongest and most profound influence happens without any kind of arm-twisting. Certainly in sales, there has to be a certain amount of persuasion, but if it is through the osmosis of influence and not the intentional power of persuasion, the results tend to last longer. Not only are they meaningful, but they also repeatable.

MOUNT RUSHMORE OF INFLUENCE

Mount Rushmore started getting carved in 1927, and it was finished in 1941. More than 3 million people a year visit the national park. The four presidents carved in granite in the Black Hills of South Dakota are George Washington, Abraham Lincoln, Thomas Jefferson, and Theodore Roosevelt. All four of these men were people of great influence. They stand tall in the mountainside and in US history.

George Washington understood the power of his purpose. He was chosen to lead a young nation and had a vision to build a great and powerful union. Thomas Jefferson was persistent as the principal author of the Declaration of Independence and eventually upheld its ideals as the third president of the United States. Abraham Lincoln needed to be persistent against all his foes while facing crises such as the Civil War, which preserved the Union and abolished slavery. Teddy Roosevelt was man who wore his passion on his sleeve and led the Progressive movement. People knew when they met him that he "walked softly but carried a big stick."

Imagine for a moment that you could commission a personal Mount Rushmore to be carved on your behalf. Who would you name as the four most influential people in your life? Who had such a monumental influence on you that the arc of your life was literally changed because of him or her? You might include a teacher, a coach, a neighbor, a friend, or even an enemy because of how he or she impacted your life. It might be someone you never met, and yet he or she had a monumental impact you. You might even find that you need to identify several Mount Rushmores for different periods of your life.

When you are able to decide who belongs on that list, try to figure out what makes these people so special. What are the traits that they all have in common? Perhaps you will detect Purpose, Persistence, and Passion in the lives of these people.

As I was trying to figure out who belonged on my list, I thought of a guy I knew in college who could be on the list because he spent his freshman year stoned. I also thought of putting a former friend's head on the monument, but they did not have room for both faces. Okay, I will admit those were both weak attempts at Mount Rushmore humor! It reminds me of the T-shirt where a couple is in the car and they look up and see the bottoms of four men sticking out of a mountain, and the husband declares, "I guess this means we must be behind Mount Rushmore." Seriously, the people on my personal Mount Rushmore are featured in this book because they aligned their values with their actions.

With some intentionality in the areas of Purpose, Persistence, and Passion, you can be on someone else's personal Mount Rushmore.

With some intentionality in the areas of Purpose, Persistence, and Passion, you can be on someone else's personal Mount Rushmore. Remember, they build monuments for people of influence, not for committees and task force groups. *Silent impact* is the key.

TIME FOR ACTION

Are you inspired but not sure what to do now? Are you ready to take some actionable steps toward making a silent impact on the world around you?

TRY SOME OF THE FOLLOWING IDEAS.

1. For the next week, make a mental note every time you hear the words *impact* or *influence*. You will be surprised to hear the different contexts in which these words are used. This will also help you "live awake" and be aware of your own influence.

2. Try making some Impact Resolutions as described on page 17. This is a great

opportunity for self-discovery and self-improvement. Be honest with yourself on areas that need improvement. It's a purpose-driven commitment that you can make to yourself.

3. Measure your impact by thinking about whose advice you would follow about a movie or restaurant (see page 25). Make mental notes on who seeks advice from you and who listens to you on minor and major things.

4. Review Pursuit of Happiness on page 70. If you want to be an influence peddler, you better make sure you are taking care of things in your own backyard. Happiness is a choice. Be pro-choice when it comes to your attitude.

5. Smile when you are on the phone (see page 85). Try to smile twice as much as you normally do and you may be surprised how people react to your positive glow. I have made more mistakes and verbal fumbles on TV than any person in local television history. When I make a mistake, I smile my way through it. It works!

6. Consider a Second Thank You as described on page 105. This can be a life-changing experience if you have the guts to do it. Make that call or write that e-mail or letter. The stories I am getting from people who have gone back to let that special person know what they did for them at a crucial moment in their lives or careers are truly inspiring. Join the Second Thank You Movement!

7. Limit your exposure to negative people. Also take a look at the words you speak. Get rid of negative words in your vocabulary. Read more on page 61.

8. For the next week, look for opportunities to lift someone's spirits. A nice comment or a compliment can change someone's day. Passion is all about showing them you care.

9. Give yourself personal pep talks. What is your trigger? Remember the story about Cris Carter on page 103? What can you say to yourself to get you over the negative thoughts that enter your mind? Before you jump out of bed in the morning, get yourself ready mentally for the challenges of the day and then relish the great moments.

10. Remember Sister Helen's secret: It's not about them feeling good about you; it's about them feeling good about themselves. Consider how you can have a silent impact on others in this way.

11. Figure out who is on your Mount Rushmore of Influence and write down why they are there. Use them to inspire you and emulate their magic. You too can have a monumental impact on others when you amplify your influence.

12. Be an IMPACT PLAYER.

ACKNOWLEDGMENTS

I'd like to start by thanking my Mount Rushmore of Influence—many of you have been featured in this book. On my wedding day, I said I was the luckiest man in the world and I still feel that way today. To my wife Laura and our amazing children, Natalie, Gaby, and Matthew, you are my heart and soul. Kids, being your dad is a privilege I do not take for granted. I am proud of you and want you to always look for ways to be a positive influence on others. Laura, you are an impact player. I am inspired by the way you have helped others find their path in life. Thank you for walking this journey with me. Thanks to my mom and dad and brothers and sisters for the way they have shaped my life. I hit the lottery with my family!

Thanks to my editor, Heidi Sheard, for her patience, guidance . . . and did I mention patience? Thanks to the designer of this book, Jay Monroe, for his creative ideas and attention to detail. I would like to thank Amy Quale and the team at Wise Ink for their expert guidance through the publishing process. To my speaking coach Juanell Teague and her assistant, Karen Brownlee, thanks for helping me find my voice and for convincing me to tell my stories and inspire people to become more influential. They also helped in my research on influence. To my many friends in the National Speakers Association who are always willing to give me advice, constructive criticism, and friendship: Ross Bernstein, Walter Bond, Jermaine Davis, David Goldman, David Horsager, Mark LeBlanc, Anna Liotta, Harvey Mackay, Mike McKinley, Cathy Paper, Sam Richter, Dr. Manny Steil, and many others. Thanks to my longtime colleagues at KSTP–TV Minneapolis–St. Paul. I am lucky to work with some very talented people on a daily basis. To all my friends, especially those who would be sitting next to me in jail, Phil Sibinski and Gary Schulzetenberg to name a couple!

ABOUT THE AUTHOR

Joe Schmit is an award-winning broadcaster, community leader, and popular keynote speaker. He has covered every major sporting event in the past three decades. He has won fifteen Emmys from the National Television Academy and a National Headliner Award. Joe is also a regular on 1500ESPN radio. Before joining KSTP–TV in Minneapolis–St. Paul in 1985, he was sports director for WBAY–TV in Green Bay, Wisconsin. His career also includes positions for KCRG–TV in Cedar Rapids, Iowa, and WKBT–TV in La Crosse, Wisconsin.

SILENT IMPACT

Joe is a longtime youth mentor committed to advocating for community organizations. He is a past president and board member of the Big Brothers and Big Sisters of Greater Twin Cities and a past president and board member of the Fairway Foundation. Joe is also a member of the PACER Advisory Board and the Minnesota Vikings Advisory Board. He and his wife, Laura, are currently chairing a $7 million capital campaign for VEAP, the largest food shelf in Minnesota. Joe earned his degree in mass communications from University of Wisconsin–La Crosse.

BOOK JOE SCHMIT
TO SPEAK AT YOUR NEXT EVENT

Want a high-energy, high-humor, high-impact presentation? Joe Schmit has delivered his Silent Impact™ keynote to hundreds of leadership groups, associations, and industry conferences. Joe's authentic style rallies audiences to embrace the power of their own influence. It's a game changer!

BREAKING NEWS!

Joe will help you . . .

- Implement impact resolutions today and see results tomorrow

- Develop a culture of innovation, accountability, and success

- Learn about the Second Thank You and Mount Rushmore of Influence

- Become aware of the power of Purpose, Persistence, and Passion

"We make our biggest impressions when we aren't trying to be impressive."

—JOE SCHMIT, SPEAKER AND AWARD-WINNING BROADCASTER

"In baseball terms, you hit a grand slam! Your Silent Impact message was spot-on with our goals. I have never before seen what happened at the end of your speech—a standing ovation. Wow!"

—MIKE GIVENS, PRESIDENT, WENDY'S/FOURCROWN INC.

"Joe's keynote was one of the finest we've ever had. He drew the audience from the start and held our attention for the whole hour as we laughed and were inspired."

—KEVIN SEISLER, MAYO COLLEGE OF MEDICINE, MAYO CLINIC

SPEECHES, BREAKOUT SESSIONS, EMCEE

To get on Joe's calendar, call **(612) 210-8463** or email Joe at **joe@joeschmit.com**.

WWW.JOESCHMIT.COM

LET'S START A MOVEMENT

Silent Impact is contagious. It's a new way of thinking. It's a new focus on how you live, work, and play. With some very simple steps, you can become a person of influence. I want to hear about your stories of influence. Tell me about something you were inspired to do that made an impact in the life of someone else. Go back and find that special person and deliver your second thank you. I want to hear your stories! Who knows, maybe you will be part of my next book. You can send them to me at **joe@joeschmit.com**.